Overleaf: *T*
on Shrove T
fairs had be
since the thi

LAVENHAM
industrial town

LAVENHAM
industrial town

by

ALEC BETTERTON

and

DAVID DYMOND

TERENCE DALTON LIMITED
LAVENHAM   .   SUFFOLK
1989

Published by

TERENCE DALTON LIMITED

ISBN 0 86138 069 X hardback
0 86138 070 3 limp covers

Originally published as
Lavenham: 700 Years of Textile Making
by The Boydell Press, 1982
This edition, revised and rewritten, 1989

Text photoset in 10/11pt Times

Printed in Great Britain at
The Lavenham Press Limited, Lavenham, Suffolk

Contents

Foreword

LAVENHAM is one of the most attractive small towns in England. Its dramatic parish church, tightly-built streets and comfortably leaning timber houses are a constant stimulus to our historical imaginations and sense of beauty. In this century several writers have laid the foundations of its history, and we especially acknowledge the pioneering work of F. Lingard Ranson and Barbara McClenaghan. Looking at their achievement, it seemed that we could best contribute by dealing more closely with the most fundamental and significant aspect of Lavenham's history, namely its strong industrial and commercial tradition, which lasted for many centuries and affected every facet of the town's life and development.

This book was first published in 1982. It came out of the work of an extra-mural class,

organized at Lavenham in 1970–74 by the Board of Extra-Mural Studies of the University of Cambridge. Because it is rooted in adult education, our writing in both editions has been aimed at two kinds of reader. First we hope that specialists and academic historians will accept it as a respectable contribution to knowledge; this is why we have endeavoured to put Lavenham into a broader setting, and given full references to all major sources of information. Secondly, and just as important, we hope that our book will be read by many people who are not specialist historians but who find endless interest in the near-perfect survival of an early town and come yearly in their thousands to discover more of its beauty and fascinating detail. This is why technical terms have been explained and academic

jargon has been studiously avoided. To widen its appeal as much as possible, this second edition has been updated, expanded and given a much larger number of illustrations.

We would like to thank Mr Peter Northeast for providing transcripts of many early wills, Dr John Pound for his transcript of the Military Survey of 1522, and Professor Donald Coleman for his warm encouragement of the project. We are also grateful to many archivists and librarians for their efficient and courteous service over many years: in particular at the Suffolk Record Office, the Public Record Office in London, and Cambridge University Library. Locally we have received much valuable help from the Lavenham Guildhall Museum Sub-committee, who have allowed us to reproduce photographs from their excellent collection. Finally we are indebted to Mr Geoff Cordy of Felixstowe for copying historical photographs, processing large numbers of prints and taking new photographs which needed a professional touch.

A note on the value of money

Sums of money recorded in historical documents are extremely difficult to relate to present-day values, especially as we live in a period of continuing inflation.

It may, of course, be helpful to compare the amounts which people earned then and now. For example, in the account book of the Howard family of Stoke-by-Nayland (1482–91) we read that "The same day my Lord paid to John How [a tiler] of Lavenham and his man

Right: *All the buildings in this view of Shilling Street about 1910 survive today, but the single-storey cottage on the right now has an upper floor. The street no longer has a bedraggled air.*

Opposite page: *Timbered buildings in Water Street. The nearest building preserves its original overhang or "jetty". Higher up the street the front walls of the ground floors have been moved forward to create a flush front in keeping with fashion from the later seventeenth century onwards.*

for four days' work 2 shillings [10p]."[1] This gives a rate of 3d a day for each person, except that John How probably took more than "his man". If, in 1989, we suppose that a bricklayer and his mate can earn a basic £200 in four days, we might be tempted to multiply all late-fifteenth century sums by 2,000 to arrive at their present equivalent. We have to remember, however, that a bricklayer's standard of living and his possessions in the fourteen-eighties bear no comparison with those of a present-day craftsman.

It must also be appreciated that in medieval and Tudor times a tremendous disparity existed between the incomes of artisans and those of successful merchants or professional men. Nicholas Bacon of Redgrave, for example, when he began to practise as a solicitor in 1537 earned £10 a year, but this soon rose to £70, then, as an attorney, to £90 and finally, as Lord Keeper, to well over £1,000 of official salary, not to mention private fees and revenues amounting to far more[2]. A multiple based on professional salaries, then and now, would be very different from one based on artisans' wages.

Rather than focusing on earnings, we may be better advised to compare the past and present prices of commodities. However, a single example can be quite misleading, for a product may be in short supply and expensive in one period but common and cheap in another.

Left: *A watchmaker's shop in High Street, 1892. In Kelly's directory of 1900 Joseph Abbott was described as watchmaker and photographer; he was still in business in 1922. His house is here decorated for a celebration by the Oddfellows.*

Opposite page: *The large timber-framed house in this view of Shilling Street has been subdivided into several cottages or "tenements". This kind of conversion was commonplace in Lavenham from the seventeenth to the nineteenth centuries.*

John Burnett has presented a study of the whole problem[3]. As he says, "Although the temptation to compare over time is irresistible . . . there can be no such thing as the value of money in the abstract. We cannot say what was the 1938 equivalent of £1 in 1338, for it depends on what one wants to buy." Nevertheless, Burnett used the index of E. H. Phelps Brown which plots the price of "a basket of consumables" over the long period from 1264 to 1954[4]. This shows that prices rose by 350% between 1475 and 1550, and by 600% by the middle of the seventeenth century. In 1954 the same commodities cost nearly fifty times more than they had in 1500. Updating these comparisons by reference to the retail cost of food, drink, fuel, light and clothing (roughly the basis of the Phelps Brown index), we find that prices in 1989 have risen to about 350 times those of 1500, ninety times those of 1550 and forty times those of 1750. But this is drastically to simplify an extremely complex situation and takes no account, for example, of the phenomenal rise in recent times of the prices of land and houses. Comparisons should always allow for changes in the standard of living, in people's needs and demands, and in the level of *real* wages[5].

1. *The Howard Household Books*. Roxburgh Club (1844), 331.
2. Alan Simpson, *The Wealth of the Gentry, 1540–1660* (1961), 62-63.
3. John Burnett, *A History of the Cost of Living* (1969).
4. E. H. Phelps Brown & Sheila V. Hopkins, "Seven Centuries of the Prices of Consumables", *Economica*, NS 23 (1956).
5. L. M. Munby, *How Much is That Worth?* (1989); this pamphlet published by the British Association for Local History will be a great help in discussing these complicated issues.

The Growth of the Cloth Industry   1

T HE MANY thousands who visit Lavenham every year are attracted by the picturesque beauty of its ancient streets and houses. It seems to exemplify the old-world English village of the calendar and picture postcard. Yet the essential historical fact is that Lavenham was once a thriving market town and one of the most important industrial and manufacturing centres in England. Far from being a rural Arcadia, Lavenham in its heyday had more in common with Victorian Leeds and Bradford, because from at least the fourteenth to the eighteenth centuries the manufacture of cloth was a major source of employment and wealth. Indeed, because the town lost its early prosperity gradually, and never adequately replaced its source, the cloth industry has largely dictated the physical appearance of the place today.

Origins and early development

The origins of the cloth industry are difficult to find. No doubt in early medieval times a certain amount of cloth was made in many villages and towns to supply purely local needs. In fact, a fuller of cloth is recorded at Hadleigh as early as about 1180[1]. Yet out of this background there must have been a trend in some areas towards a specialist industry which could supply wider markets. It is certain that such a specialization had emerged in southern

Suffolk by the early fourteenth century. Our best evidence lies in the local returns for a national tax, or Lay Subsidy, which was levied in 1327[2].

For each township the tax collectors listed the names of all taxpayers and the amounts they paid. As surnames had not yet become fully hereditary, they are therefore evidence of the lives of their bearers or of their immediate predecessors. Several categories of surnames exist, but here we are primarily interested in those which imply a person's occupation. Of the forty-three names listed for Lavenham, eleven were occupational. They included a butler, a smith, a shepherd and a miller, but the other seven, a highly significant proportion, were all connected with the manufacture of cloth. Three families were called le Webbe (weaver), one Tixtor (Latin for weaver), one Fullon (a fuller who thickens cloth), one Cissor (a shearman who cuts the nap of cloth) and one Dyer. Admittedly some local surnames were already hereditary by 1327, as shown by the fact that Johannes le Webbe was further described as Cissor, but this does not necessarily reduce the value of the evidence; it merely shows that the industry has roots which go back a generation or two earlier, into the thirteenth century at least[3].

The subsidy of 1327 also affords us the opportunity of seeing how such occupational surnames were distributed in Suffolk as a whole. The eight most important surnames

1

implying a connection with cloth (Webbe, Webbere,Webbestere, Textor, Dyer, Tinctor, Cissor and Fuller) occurred sixty-five times throughout the county. Of these no fewer than twenty-eight, or 43%, were listed under the administrative hundreds of Babergh and Cosford, yet these two adjacent areas between them made up less than 10% of the total acreage of Suffolk. In these two hundreds lie most of the centres which were later to become famous for cloth, for example Sudbury, Glemsford, Long Melford, Boxford, Hadleigh, Nayland, Stoke-by-Nayland and Lavenham

Lavenham Hall stands on the site of the principal medieval manor house. From the eleventh to the sixteenth centuries this manor was owned by the de Veres, Earls of Oxford. The pond feeds a watercourse which flows down Water Street.

itself. By 1327 Babergh and Cosford had already become a specialist manufacturing district, and the economic character of local villages and market towns had changed[4]. These trends were set well before 1337 when Edward III invited Flemish weavers into England. The importance of this decision has certainly been exaggerated in the past, and no evidence has been found in the fourteenth century to connect Flemish weavers with Lavenham[5].

These early developments leave us with a more fundamental problem. Why did the cloth industry develop particularly strongly in this district? Joan Thirsk has argued that no one reason can be completely satisfying. Local wool did not make a cloth industry, for, as Thomas Fuller rightly observed, counties like Leicestershire, Lincolnshire, Northamptonshire and Cambridgeshire,"who had most of

Lavenham
... a stroll through history

by

Peter Rushton

Lavenham

I watch the ancient weavers, hear their speech
  as quaint and flavoured as old Shakespeare knew:
the great beamed halls lean over, each to each;
  a hundred sheep go blindly bleating through
the cobbled thoroughfare; the gossips throng
  screaming their ribald chatter to the sky;
coaches and horses loudly clack along;
  starveling apprentices go running by.

Where are they now, the folk who made this place
  alive with warmth and love? How still it lies;
only the tourist's interested face
  looks on its artefacts with curious eyes.

So much of Suffolk - yet so little left.
I walk out of my dream - and feel bereft.

Stefanie Fone

Lavenham – The Guildhall

Lavenham
... a stroll through history

by

Peter Rushton

Lavenham, widely regarded as being one of the finest surviving examples of a medieval town, was founded on the wool trade, which brought prosperity to the population in the fifteenth and sixteenth centuries. And prosperity there was, in those days. In 1397, when King Richard ll demanded a loan from the seventy wealthiest towns in the land, Lavenham had to pay up as it stood fifty second on the list ranking equally with Bath, Derby and Plymouth. A hundred and twenty odd years later it lay fourteenth, and the magnificent church and exquisite houses of the era are mute testament to the town's importance.

Why the wool trade evolved and prospered to the extent that it did is not clear, but local historians suggest that the manorial system, ostensibly feudalistic in nature, nevertheless gave people the opportunity to develop their own livlihood as they saw fit.

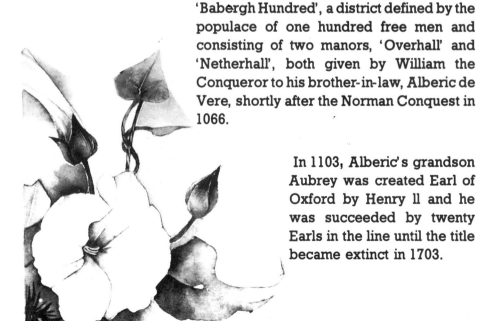

In Saxon times Lavenham was part of the 'Babergh Hundred', a district defined by the populace of one hundred free men and consisting of two manors, 'Overhall' and 'Netherhall', both given by William the Conqueror to his brother-in-law, Alberic de Vere, shortly after the Norman Conquest in 1066.

In 1103, Alberic's grandson Aubrey was created Earl of Oxford by Henry ll and he was succeeded by twenty Earls in the line until the title became extinct in 1703.

In 1257 Lavenham was given its first Market Charter and less than a century later records show that the town had already become a centre for cloth making. Initially, the English cloth industry was concerned with the export of raw wool to its Flemish counterpart but in the thirteen hundreds many Flemish weavers emigrated to England, some settling, perhaps, in Lavenham.

It was from this time that the town's great involvement with wool began.

Primarily a cottage industry, the trade was controlled by the few who held the reins of power and wealth and they formed themselves into Guilds. Often thought of as craft organisations the Guilds were, in fact, religious institutions. Four existed in the town: the Guilds of Corpus Christie, Holy Trinity, Our Lady and Saints Peter and Paul. Each Guild built for itself a meeting place and since membership was extensive, these needed to be quite large, with cooking, storage and meeting facilities. Two of the Guildhalls survive in Lavenham - those of the Guild of Corpus Christie and the Guild of Our Lady. The latter, now known as 'The Wool Hall' is an integral part of The Swan Hotel, will be discussed in greater detail a little later.

LAVENHAM, SUFFOLK
– THE GUILDHALL

LADY STREET

P.P. Rushton
Feb. 1984

The Guildhall of Corpus Christie, which dominates the market place and is well known to recipients of Lavenham postcards, was completed in about 1529 for the Guild which had been established by charter from John de Vere, 15th Earl of Oxford.

The Guild was to be shortlived, suffering the same fate as other religious organisations dissolved by Acts of Parliament in 1545 and 1547, but thankfully the building survived.

Today its exterior remains much as it was when first built, distinctive by the mass of timber used in its construction and a supreme example of a close-studded timber framed building.

Rampant lions carved on the doorposts of the porch were the emblem of the Guild, and the carved figure on the cornerpost is said to represent the Earl of Oxford. Over the centuries the Guildhall has had a chequered history. In 1555 during the Marian persecutions, Dr. Rowland Taylor, Rector of Hadleigh, was imprisoned here before being burned at the stake on Aldham common where his grave can still be seen; in 1596 the building was acquired by the parish and was used as a town hall for almost a century; by the mid-sixteen hundreds it had become a House of Correction and successively has been a workhouse, almshouse and wool store. Today it houses an excellent museum, run by the National Trust in conjuction with the local community, and this is open at advertised times. Behind the Guildhall is a delightful walled garden and the restored 19th Century Parish lock-up and Mortuary.

The Wool Hall, on the corner of Water and Lady Streets, has an interesting recent history, for in 1911 it was almost lost to Lavenham for good. At that time it was fashionable to dismantle timber-framed and other 'quaint' buildings in small towns and move them to the estates of the wealthy. Some of Lavenham's buildings suffered this fate, including one which was taken to the sea-front at Clacton. The Wool Hall was destined for a similar end. The timbers were carefully marked to facilitate re-erection on the Ascot Estates of Princess Louise, and demolition commenced. By the time the pieces were loaded onto wagons for the journey south, the appalled locals organised themselves to prevent removal. Reputedly, the Reverend Taylor led the revolt and, mounted on his bicycle with robes flying, chased after the disappearing vehicles and presented a petition to the Princess, begging her to return the Hall. She agreed, with the stipulation that the re-erected building be used as a convalescent home for the womenfolk of railwaymen. So it was that the beautiful building, now the only representative example of an ancient wool hall, was restored to the town.

But it is not only the Guildhalls that testify to bygone wealth. Fine buildings abound everywhere, with the local skyline dominated by the tower of Lavenham's Parish Church of Saint Peter and Saint Paul. The biggest financial contributor to the church's construction was a wealthy wool merchant called Thomas Spring lll. He and John de Vere, Earl of Oxford and brilliant commander of part of Henry Vll's forces, collaborated to celebrate the latter's safe and victorious return to Lavenham from the Battle of Bosworth. Their collaboration spawned the Late Perpendicular style building which was completed in 1525. The very size of the church reflectes the wealth and gratitude of its benefactors: the building is 191 feet long and 68 feet wide, and the tower soars 141 feet into the Suffolk sky. The emblems and coats of arms of the Spring and de Vere families may be found carved many times into the fabric of the building whilst the Spring Parclose, in the body of the church itself, is a most splendid memorial to the family who gave so much to both church and town. The tower houses the Lavenham bells, well known in bell-ringing circles. The tenor bell, described as 'the finest toned bell in England, probably the world' was cast in 1625 by the famous bell-founder Miles Graye.

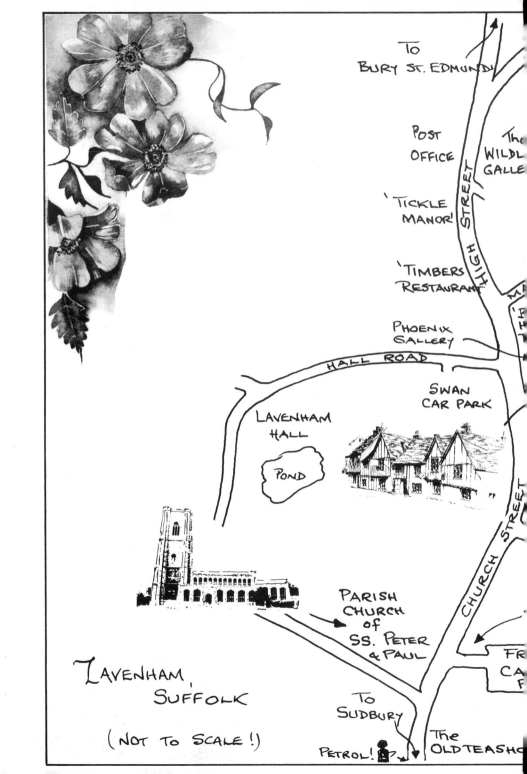

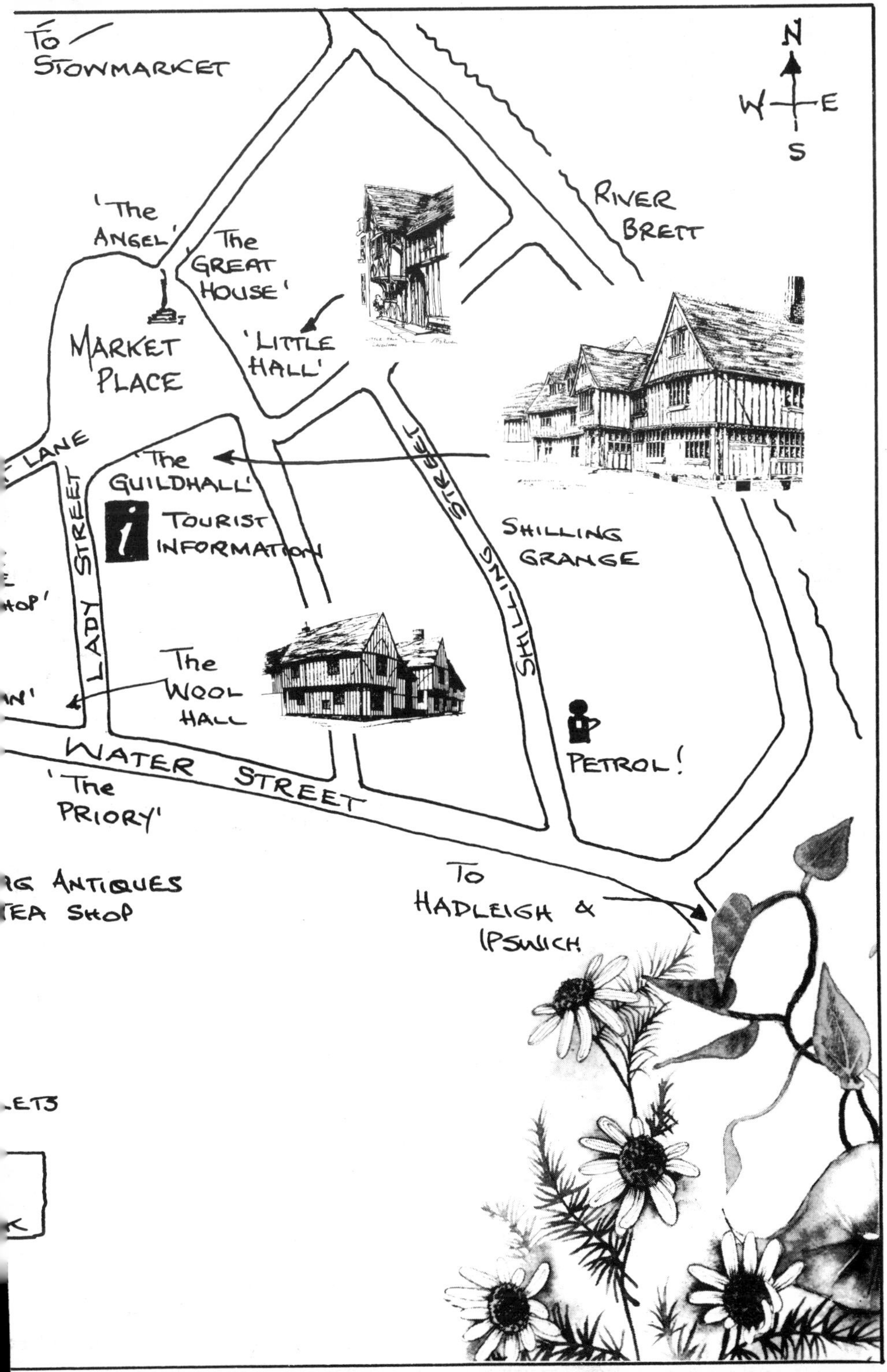

To
STOWMARKET

N
W E
S

'The
ANGEL'

The
GREAT
HOUSE'

RIVER
BRETT

MARKET
PLACE

'LITTLE
HALL'

LANE

LADY STREET

'The
GUILDHALL'

_i_ TOURIST
INFORMATION

SHILLING STREET

SHILLING
GRANGE

'OP'

N'

The
WOOL
HALL

PETROL!

WATER STREET

'The
PRIORY'

To
HADLEIGH &
IPSWICH

G ANTIQUES
TEA SHOP

ET3

K

Other buildings of note are Shilling Grange in Shilling Street, built by clothier John Shilling in the 15th Century. In the 1780s the house was the home of engraver Issac Taylor, whose daughter Jane wrote the endearing nursery rhyme 'Twinkle, Twinkle, Little Star', perhaps in this house! Another is the de Vere House in Water Street where carvings of the family emblems, the star and boar, may be seen. Almost next door is The Priory, which has been painstakingly restored by its present owners in recent years, and is open to the public at advertised times.

LITTLE HALL
LAVENHAM

P.D. Rushton

In the market place may be found Little Hall which dates back to the fifteenth century. Once the home of the Causton family, today this fine hall house is the headquarters of The Suffolk Preservation Society, and is open to the public from Easter to mid-October. The magnificent crown post roof is worth seeing.

THE SWAN ~ LAVENHAM, SUFFOLK

The market place itself is quite unusual because of its location: in most towns and villages it is an integral part of the High Street, but here it stands alone, quite separate from that thoroughfare. In the fifteenth century it was called The Forum. A rich clothier called William Jacob, who lived, perhaps, in Molet House in Barn Street directed in his will of 1500 that ' a cross made at my proper cost be set in the Market Hill in Lavenham, the pattern to be the cross standing in Cambridge Market Place'. The base of Jacob's cross still stands, but the original shaft has not survived, nor has the Cambridge model, making comparison impossible.

Lavenham's famous blue cloth gave rise to the term 'dyed in the wool', for the raw wool was dyed in woad before being woven. It is interesting to note that villains practiced their art even in those days, for in 1592 one Roger Ruggles was charged with dying his wool with logwood, an inferior blue dye which was forbidden by law!

Different shades of blue were achieved by varying the concentration of the dye. Some red cloth was also produced, a very expensive version dyed in dye made from the body of a particular insect, with a cheaper version produced from a dye made of madder, in the fourteenth century grown in nearby Great Waldingfield.

Three main types of cloth were made in Suffolk - broadcloths, narrow cloths and 'streytes', the latter half the length, half the width and a quarter of the weight of broadcloth, which itself was required by statute to be 28 yards and 28 inches long, five feet three inches broad, and 38 pounds in weight. In Lavenham, the emphasis was on weaving broadcloth, with surrounding towns and villages producing different types.

WINING and DINING.

This little book does not attempt to list all the many worthy hostelries in the town - hungry and thirsty travellers will find these for themselves. But it would be unworthy not to mention a few.

Perhaps the focal point of the High Street is 'The Swan Hotel', (pictured on page 11) which owes its very existence to the prosperity of the wool era. The three houses from which the hotel has developed are recorded from 1425, and the oldest part bears traces of late fourteenth century workmanship. Well established as an inn by 1667 when John Girling, the then landlord issued a 'Trader's Token', the Swan continued to flourish and by 1830 had stabling for fifty horses, being as it was, by then a 'capital old-established free public and posting house'. In the seventeen hundreds, the coach known as 'The Lavenham Machine' ran a thrice weekly service between

Lavenham and 'The Spread Eagle' in London's Gracechurch Street, probably collecting travellers from 'The Swan' before departing Lavenham at five o'clock in the morning every Monday, Wednesday and Friday.

Today 'The Swan' is owned by Forte, and is a truly lovely hotel, offering great antiquity and atmosphere combined with superb comfort and excellent cuisine.

Opposite the church is 'The Old Teashop', where visitors can enjoy a break and a delicious cream tea amidst the beams and thatch of this pretty example of a Suffolk cottage, whilst further along the High Street will be found 'The Bankhouse Teashop', 'Timbers Restaurant' and 'The Tickle Manor Teashop'.

Antique lovers can enjoy a range of refreshments in 'Flags Tea Shop', whilst they browse amongst the antiques.

The 'Great House Hotel and Restaurant' in the market place may be described as 'a little corner of France nestling in medieval England', for here may be found the most delightful cuisine, lovingly prepared and served in the best of French traditions. Superb accommodation with all facilities is on offer, and the establishment is widely recommended in all the main guides.

Next door is 'The Angel Inn' offering freshly cooked lunches and evening meals, and a menu that is changed daily. En-suite accommodation, at very reasonable rates, is also available.

'The Greyhound' is an olde worlde village inn serving morning coffee, bar lunches and evening meals, whilst visitors to 'The Priory' can partake of delicious lunches and Suffolk Cream Teas in the Refectory Restaurant.

TOURIST INFORMATION

A new Tourist Information Centre has recently been opened in Lady Street, a few doors down from the market place, and here visitors can avail themselves of a wealth of information on Lavenham and its surrounding towns and villages.

Acknowledgements:

Stefanie Fone, for her poem 'Lavenham'
Juliette Clarke, for her cover illustration
Hugh Mansell, for his line drawing of 'The Great House'
Rosemary Rushton, for her idea and boundless enthusiasm.

Printed and published by
KINDAIM LTD.,
Stowmarket, Suffolk IP14 1NN

Kindaim
LIMITED

Printed and published by
KINDAIM LTD.,
Stowmarket, Suffolk IP14 1NN

© Kindaim Ltd., 1993

wool, had least of clothing"[6]. In fact Suffolk wool was considered inferior to that of most other counties. Neither was fuller's earth to be found in the Suffolk clothing district. The existence of a local port does not seem to be vital, for even West Country cloth went by road to be marketed at Blackwell Hall in London[7]. A supply of running water, on the other hand, was very necessary, but this alone did not make a cloth centre[8].

Evidence is hard to come by. The factors favouring economic growth must have been partly technological (here the development of the fulling mill in the thirteenth century may have been significant) but mainly human. There had to be enough people who needed new sources of employment, full-time or part-time. The thirteenth and early fourteenth centuries were certainly a period of great population pressure, and this made agricultural land an increasingly scarce commodity. Manorial customs of inheritance and personal decisions had the effect of dividing farms into units hardly large enough to support a family, and thereby drove people to seek supplementary employment. A link certainly existed between farming and clothmaking. Thirsk has cited the case of the early cloth industry in rural Wiltshire whose location was identical with that of the county's dairy farms[9]. The wills of many clothiers from Lavenham, even prosperous ones, show that a stake in agriculture was invariably retained, and perhaps positively increased. For example, in 1440 John Place, a wealthy clothier who lived in High Street, bequeathed not only "all my woollen cloth and my white wool and blue and yarn" but also three horses, grain sown and unsown, a cart and a tumbrel. Similarly, in 1473 John Harry, who lived nearby in the same street, left wheat, malt and two cows as well as wool and cloths[10].

Another necessary ingredient was sufficient personal freedom to pursue new patterns of work. Paradoxically this was found more easily in rural areas like Babergh, where manorial lords had a more liberal attitude towards new industrial developments, than in established towns where early clothmaking had tended to

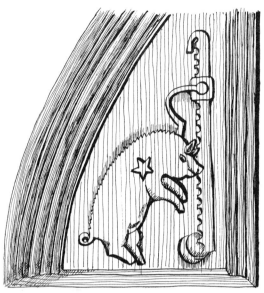

Symbols of a great family on the south door of the church. The de Veres used several symbols including the boar (Latin verris, a pun on Vere), a five-pointed star, and a mechanical pot-hook or jack (because, allegedly, most of the male de Veres in the Tudor period had the Christian name John).

be stifled by the growth of regulations and restrictive practices. From Norman times the powerful de Vere family, Earls of Oxford, were lords of the principal manor of Lavenham. Although their main residence was over the Essex border at Hedingham, where the massive keep of their castle still survives, they had at Lavenham a hunting park to the north of the town and a manor house near the church. This family had clearly stimulated Lavenham's growth in the thirteenth century from an agricultural village to a market town. In 1257 a market charter was acquired from the Crown, while in 1329 the Earl and his tenants in Lavenham were granted exemption from tolls on all goods throughout the realm[11]. It is tempting to suppose that the de Veres similarly encouraged the cloth industry in its formative years. Although it was larger than many an incorporated borough, and indeed called itself a borough and its inhabitants burgesses,

Lavenham was never governed by a mayor and corporation. Administratively it remained a large, manorialized "village" with charters for only a weekly market and two annual fairs. Its daily life was controlled by six headboroughs who were appointed by the lord of the manor[12]. The thick scatter of such chartered markets in southern Suffolk could have been an important factor in the growth of the cloth trade: such places already had a climate which encouraged personal initiative and the development of specialized crafts and trades[13].

By the end of the fourteenth century Lavenham's role as a clothmaking centre is clearer. For example, in October, 1358, the Crown granted commissions to various people throughout the country to collect a complicated subsidy on cloth for sale; the two men appointed to cover Essex were William de Lambourn and Alan Hunte, both of Lavenham[14]. This shows that the town already had reserves of expertise in cloth which were nationally recognized. When in 1397 "loans" were demanded by the Crown from seventy of the more important towns of England, Lavenham was well placed among them and paid the same as Bath, Derby, Lichfield and Ply-

mouth[15]. In the Patent Rolls of this period (1390–1420) can be found a dozen or more references to Lavenham businessmen, for the most part concerning sums of money owed to them, and sometimes by them[16]. For example on 4th February, 1390, Hervey de Lackford had failed to meet a debt of £12 to John Carpenter of Lavenham. When he died in 1416 Carpenter was a prosperous man: he owned several properties in the town, one with a dovecote, kept cows and a flock of sheep, and had a woadhouse or dyehouse in the High Street still referred to in later wills as "Carpenter's Dyehouse". All this reflects the growing volume of cloth trading, which can also be seen on a county scale in the earliest surviving aulnage accounts—a sort of tax levied on saleable cloths[17].

After 1400 there begins a period which is much better documented. In particular a remarkable number of wills helps us to plot the town's rising prosperity through the fifteenth century to a peak in the first half of the sixteenth, when it was one of the richest towns in England and recognized as a foremost manufacturing centre. Moreover, we can attribute this status unquestionably and almost

Opposite page: *The Market Place and William Jacob's cross early this century. The buildings to the left of the cross had encroached on the Market Place, hiding the Corpus Christi Gildhall; they were demolished in 1938. On the extreme left is the nonconformist British School, built in 1861, which survived to celebrate its centenary before being pulled down.*

Right: *The Horse Fair in the High Street in the late nineteenth century. The entrance to Market Street can be seen on the left. The lower end of the street is greatly congested.*

exclusively to the making and trading of its famous woollen cloth.

Wills of this period were proved, with few exceptions, in one of three types of ecclesiastical court. Generally speaking, only 10% or less of the population left wills anyway, and of these the majority were proved in the local archdeacon's court. Some of the more important people, including the clergy, had their wills proved at a higher level in the bishop's or consistory court. A third category, usually the wealthiest who possessed property in more than one diocese, had their wills proved higher still in the prerogative court of the archdiocese—in Lavenham's case, of Canterbury. These are referred to as PCC wills. The graph of all known Lavenham wills proved between 1360 and 1660 shows a prodigious rise about the turn of the fifteenth and sixteenth centuries

both in the number of PCC wills (those of the richest) and in their proportion of the total. This must reflect a massive boom in Lavenham's industry and wealth.

The same pattern arises from the incidence *(number)* and lavishness of bequests to the parish church and for the repair of highways (see p.16). Wealthy businessmen also invested their fortunes in lands and houses, as is shown by the rising numbers of properties bequeathed in wills; but this is less reliable evidence than other forms of bequest because the size and value of properties is not mentioned and can rarely be accurately deduced.

The wills of those known to have been involved in clothmaking are of special interest. Although the occupation of testators is not always mentioned, the evidence we have is powerfully significant. Of the 102 known wills

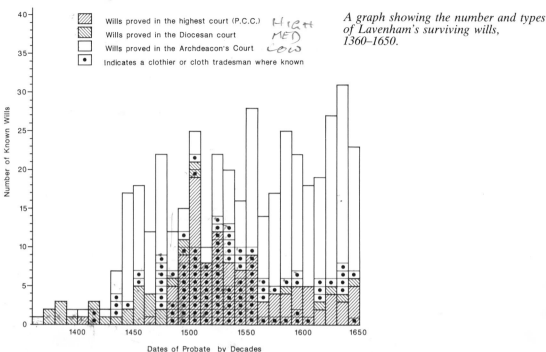

A graph showing the number and types of Lavenham's surviving wills, 1360–1650.

Number of Known Wills

Dates of Probate by Decades

of the period before 1490, only twenty testators can be positively connected with cloth (20%), yet of the 135 wills proved between 1490 and 1560 as many as eighty-five testators (63%) are known to have been involved with the industry. The upward surge of Lavenham's wealth is exactly matched by the rising number of its clothmakers' wills.

In 1522 Lavenham boasted at least nineteen occupations apart from those involved with cloth (see p. 41)[18]. Out of this array only a few priests, butchers, tanners and cordwainers (leatherworkers) seem to have been prosperous enough to make proper written wills, though admittedly a few other groups may be concealed in wills which omit the testator's occupation. A clear exception, however, was the Joly family, who with their stalls in the Market Place certainly made a good living out of butchering. The importance of the provision market must never be forgotten, because for centuries it provided a basic economic service to the whole community. The sale of meat and grain was no doubt a regular feature, but

occasionally we hear of more unexpected commodities. In 1419, for example, the steward of Dame Alice de Bryene of nearby Acton Hall bought one and a quarter barrels of salmon at Lavenham for 20s, and a quarter-barrel of sturgeon for 14s[19].

Further evidence of Lavenham's growing prosperity in the fifteenth century appears in the accounts of officials appointed by the Crown and known as aulnagers. A subsidy was imposed on cloths offered for sale and a small fee, known as aulnage, for sealing each cloth. On every broadcloth, for example, a subsidy of 4d was charged, plus an aulnage of ½d. The accounts often record the name of each clothier, the number of cloths he submitted and the amount of subsidy and aulnage he paid. Dr Gladys Thornton, in a pioneering piece of economic history published in 1928, showed that the accounts were a genuine reflection of business activity until about 1473[20]. Thereafter, they were either copied from earlier figures or simply fabricated by those who rented the office of aulnager.

In the fourteen-sixties, when Suffolk was a leading cloth-exporting county, the accounts show that Lavenham was producing substantially more than any other Suffolk community except Hadleigh. But figures for Hadleigh sometimes included places as distant as Boxford and Needham Market, whereas Lavenham invariably stood alone. In the year 1468–69, for example, 1,001½ broadcloths were made in Lavenham, more than were produced by Melford, the Waldingfields, Sudbury, Glemsford and Clare put together, while Hadleigh with Bildeston produced 1,707. Meanwhile, Bury St Edmunds made 644 broadcloths; Dedham in Essex with East Bergholt and Stratford St Mary made 531; Ipswich, with contributions from as far away as Bungay, Beccles and Halesworth, could muster only 522. The only other community in East Anglia which could outproduce Lavenham was Colchester, which with St Osyth's accounted for 1,390 broadcloths.

Six out of ten annual accounts survive for Lavenham in the fourteen-sixties, giving names of producers and a total of cloths per person, but they have obvious faults. For example, two of them refer to periods of less than a year; at least two different aulnagers were involved; some names are written inaccurately; and aulnagers may not always have listed the same kinds of cloth. Nevertheless, some interesting conclusions can be hazarded. Over the decade, at least seventy-one individuals are named as producers of cloth in Lavenham. The great majority are likely to be local residents, though some may have been "outsiders". Already prominent were several family names which were to dominate Lavenham's industry in the reigns of Henry VII and Henry VIII, such as Braunche, Grome, Jacob and Sexteyn.

Most of the named producers appear irregularly, and their annual production oscillates unpredictably. Only five individuals appeared on all six accounts: John Hary, William Jacob, John Newman, Alan Sexteyn and Thomas Spring II. By contrast thirty-four people (48%) appeared only once, and another twenty-four (34%) appeared only intermittently. Altogether, 5,148 broadcloths were taxed, in annual quantities ranging from one to 200 cloths. Only 45% of the total output came in annual batches exceeding fifty cloths, and much of the work was clearly done on a relatively small scale. Nor were the highest annual totals necessarily produced by those who contributed most regularly. For example,

PRODUCTION OF CLOTH IN LAVENHAM, 1463–64 [from Aulnage Accounts: PRO, E101/342.21]	
No of cloths	Names of clothiers
49	Thomas Spryng
38	Simon Braunche
38	William Jacob
36	John Newman
34	Robert Grom
33	Alexander Sexteyn
32	John Wylymot
29	Roger Critot
26	John Hary
22	John Baker
22	Henry Pulco
18	John Goslyn
18	Simon Trewe
17	John Sawier
14	Alan Dexter
14	William Saier (?)
13	Nicholas Gosby
13	John Lynche
11	Edward Beco—
11	Edward Clog
10	Agnes Spryng
10	William Spryng
9	Robert Wylymot
8	Simon Beryne
6	John Shelton
5	Robert Parle
5	John Pyg
5	Thomas Stoke
3	Thomas Beryne
3	William Clog
2	Janyn de eadem
1	Nicholas Blome
555 cloths	32 clothiers

PRODUCTION OF CLOTH IN LAVENHAM, 1468–69 [from Aulnage Accounts: PRO, E101/343.5]	
No of broad cloths	Names of clothiers
200	Roger Creketot
80	John Shelton
80	Thomas Spryng
80	William Jacob
70	John Rysby
70	Robert Parle
60½	John Harry
60	Alan Sexteyn
50	Edmund Bowde
40	John Barton
40	Thomas Bereve
30½	John Cook
30	Simon Braunche
16	Robert Welymot
15	Wife of John Grygges
14	John Smyth
13	Thomas Stoke
12½	Alan Dexter
6	Henry Basse
2½	John Newman
1½	Laurence Toffyle
30	From various outsiders bringing cloth, within the jurisdiction of this township
1,001½ cloths	21+ clothiers

out of six annual totals exceeding 100 cloths, only one belonged to a regular contributor[20a].

The account for 1465–66 is unusually divided into two "terms". Out of forty-three producers twenty-one contributed in the Easter term only, twelve contributed to both terms, and ten to the Michaelmas term only. This seems to underline the seasonal nature of the trade, for some people are likely to have put their farming first and turned to clothmaking only in the winter months. Moreover, thirty-two of seventy-one individuals listed in this decade shared a surname, and often registered their cloths in different years: that suggests team-work within families. To summarize, although a few specialists were undoubtedly emerging in the fourteen-sixties, most clothiers operated intermittently or even occasionally, and probably combined clothmaking with farming or other commercial pursuits[20b].

Rebuilding the church

In any reconstruction of life in Lavenham, the parish church is vital evidence. Indeed this rich building presents more impressively than any graph the rising fortunes of the early Tudor

Below: *A carved frieze running around the ceiling of the Spring Chantry in the church displays the coat of arms and initials of Thomas Spring III, who died in 1523.*

town. From about 1485 the greater part of the church was magnificently rebuilt as the clothiers' fortunes grew. It was completed in the fifteen-twenties, at the peak of the town's wealth and fame. The high standard of craftsmanship was undoubtedly expensive, and so were the building materials. For example, the nave and aisles are built almost entirely of costly limestone which had to be transported from Lincolnshire or Northamptonshire, whereas most of the other great Perpendicular churches of East Anglia relied heavily on local flint. With its proud display of personal symbols, coats of arms, merchants' marks and inscriptions, this famous building seems as much a monument to man's worldliness as to his piety.

If the interior of the church had been treated with greater respect after the Reformation, we should have learned much more about local society in the later Middle Ages. For example, about a score of brasses and inscriptions have been destroyed, leaving merely their tantalizing outlines or "indents" on the floor. Nor is the documentary record particularly good. The neighbouring parish of Long Melford has a detailed list of its church's embellishments which was written in 1529, and a remarkable description of what the church looked like before the Reformation, but Lavenham unfortunately has no such advantages[21].

Nevertheless, details mentioned in wills give us some precious glimpses of the church's interior and of the fittings, images, plate and vestments which once matched the fabric. Apart from the high altar, which was draped in gold cloth and furnished with a canopy, other altars were dedicated to St Mary, St Thomas, St Katherine and St Christopher. Images housed in carved tabernacles depicted those saints as well as St James, St Peter, St Paul, St John, St Anthony, St Anne, Our Lady of Pity and Our Lady of the Five Joys. A "great image of the crucifix" was supported by the roodbeam and on the roodloft was an organ; a handsome sum was also left for what must have been a magnificent candlebeam. The font had been given an expensive cover. Money was regularly bequeathed for the gilding and painting of all these furnishings, and in one case for "a silver and gilt crown for the image of Our Lady, the which is worshipped with divers oblations". Candles burned continually before the images, and plenty of money was left to buy wax.

Behind a few individuals like the Springs, de Veres and Braunches who were wealthy enough to commemorate their contributions by leaving their names and devices on the stone fabric, hundreds of other people were no less interested in the great rebuilding of Lavenham church. Wills, although they represent less than 10% of the population, yield a total of forty-nine bequests made specifically to the fabric of the church during its rebuilding. Many of these bequests came from families who were much less prosperous than the top dozen or so.

Lavenham was distinguished at this time by having as the lord of its principal manor the celebrated John de Vere, 13th Earl of Oxford. He was a former Constable of England, a brilliant and successful commander at the

One of eight bosses forming a canopy above the rood screen in the parish church bears the merchant mark of the Spring family.

9

battles of Barnet and Bosworth, and lately Lord Great Chamberlain, officiating at the coronation of Henry VII and Elizabeth of York. In his will he contributed only a relatively modest £20 to Lavenham church[22], but in his lifetime he had given the same amount and had inspired the vast programme of rebuilding by heading some kind of sub-scription fund. Other potential subscribers had clearly come under pressure from the Earl, as their wills reveal. The clothier William Jacob in 1500 left "to the church of Lavenham £20—the which £20 I granted before my Lord of Oxenford". In 1501 Elizabeth Braunche left "to the reparation of the church of Lavenham, as I promised to my Lord of Oxenford, 100 marks in money, of which 100 marks I have delivered and paid beforehand by the hands of the collectors of the said church £10". John Newton, another clothier, in his will dated

---

WILL OF THOMAS SPRING I, 1440

[SRO(B), 19 Baldwyne]

[Translated from Latin]

In the name of God Amen, the sixteenth day of June 1440, I Thomas Spryng of Lavenham, whole of mind, make my testament in this manner. First, I leave my soul to Almighty God my creator, to the Blessed Virgin Mary and to all His saints, and my body to be buried in the cemetery of the church of Lavenham aforesaid. Item, I leave to the high altar of the same church for tithes and oblations forgotten 40 shillings. Item, I leave to the fabric of the aforesaid church 100 shillings. Item, I leave to Agnes my wife my capital tenement in which I live, with a certain messuage adjacent called Presthows, with all its appurtenances, to hold to the same Agnes and her assigns for the term of her life. And I wish that after the death of the same Agnes the said tenement with appurtenances may remain to Thomas my son and his heirs, unless the aforesaid Agnes is truly forced by need to alienate the said tenement in her lifetime. Item, I leave to the aforesaid Agnes all the utensils and necessaries of my house. I leave to the said Agnes £100 of money to be raised from my goods and debts. Item, I leave to Thomas my aforesaid son my tenement in Preston with appurtenances, lately of John Hogon, to hold to the same Thomas and his heirs of the chief [lords], etc. Item, I leave to Katherine my daughter my tenement with appurtenances in Lavenham aforesaid in the street called Maystyrionstrete,[1] lately of John Shepperd, clerk, to hold to the same Katherine and her heirs. Item, I leave to my son William my tenement with appurtenances in Lavenham lying in Boltonstrete, lately of John Person, to hold to the same William and his heirs. Item, I leave to the same William from my said goods and chattels £20. Item, I leave to Dionisia[2] my daughter my tenement with appurtenances in Lavenham lying in the street Prentyestrete, lately of John Place, to hold to the same Dionisia and her heirs. Item, I leave to the aforesaid Dionisia from my goods and chattels £20. Item, I leave for one priest to say divine service in the church of Lavenham for the health of my soul for four years a suitable stipend, at the discretion of my executors. Item, I leave to distribute to twelve paupers each Wednesday twelve pence, during a term of four years after my death. Item, I leave to the repair of the King's highway between Lavenham and Bury St Edmunds 9 marks. The rest of my goods and chattels not bequeathed I give and leave to my executors that they may fulfil my present will faithfully, pay the debts which I owe, and therefrom dispose for the health of my soul and my parents' [souls], as by their discretion it shall seem better to do. Indeed, as my executors I make and appoint the aforesaid Agnes my wife, Geoffrey Fermer, William Curby and John Cobold. Item, I leave to each of them for his work 40 shillings. In witness of which things, etc.

[Proved at Cockfield, 8th Feb. 1440]

1   That is, Master John Street.
2   Denyse, in modern parlance.

1502 directed "Margery my wife to pay to the church of Lavenham the residue of the money that I owe *by my promise*, that is £1 6s 8d"[23].

The Earl was an opportunist. When the clothier Thomas Risby died in 1500, bequeathing sums totalling over £400 as well as six landed properties, the Earl was appointed supervisor of the will, receiving a lavish £40 for his pains; Thomas' son John appears then to have misappropriated from the sale of his father's goods considerable sums of money which, on John's own death in 1504, the Earl was able to channel into the church building fund. On his deathbed John Risby hastily directed that "in discharging of his conscience and his soul . . . for certain goods that he hath sold of his father's and hath appropriated . . . £200 of the said goods of his father's should be

Elaborately rebuilt (apart from the chancel) from about 1450 onwards, Lavenham Church is one of England's finest parish churches. The last part to be erected, from 1486 to c1525, though never properly finished with pinnacles, was the noble tower, 141 feet high.

disposed to the edifying of Lavenham church . . . by the advice and oversight of my lord of Oxford"[24].

Another useful contribution to the building of the tower was exacted by the parson in 1521 in settlement of a quarrel between the clothier Symond Causton and the sons of his brother William. The parson, Dr Thomas Stockhouse, was appointed arbiter. Symond Causton's will asked his executors to "pay to the building of

11

WILL OF THOMAS SPRING II, 1486

[PRO, PCC 25 Logge]

[Translated from Latin]

In the name of God Amen, 29th March 1486, I Thomas Spring of Lavenham in the diocese of Norwich, whole of mind and of perfect memory, make my testament in this manner. First, I leave my soul to Almighty God, and my body to be buried in the vestry [*in vestibulo*] of the parish church of the Blessed Apostle Peter of Lavenham. Item, I leave to William Spring my son £100 of legal English money. Item, I leave to James my son £100 of legal English money. Item, I leave to Marion my daughter £100 of legal English money. Item, I leave to the Rector of my parish 10 shillings that he may pray for my soul. Item, I leave to my spinners, fullers and weavers [*filatriabus fullonibus & textoribus*] 100 marks to be distributed among them according to the discretion of my executors. Item, I leave to the building of the bell-tower [*campanil'*], in English 'stepyll', of the parish church of Lavenham aforesaid 300 marks. Item, I wish that my executors may find a suitable priest to celebrate masses for my soul for twenty years in the parish church of Lavenham aforesaid. Item, I leave for the repair of broken roads around Lavenham 200 marks. Item, I leave to the Franciscan friars [*fratribus ordinis minorum*] of Babwell[1] 20 marks. Item, I leave to the Dominican friars [*fratribus ordinis fratrum predicatorum*] of Sudbury 20 marks. Item, I leave to the Austin friars [*fratribus ordinis Augustinencis*] of Clare 10 marks. However, the rest of my goods not bequeathed above I give and leave to Margaret my wife and Thomas Spring my eldest son, whom I appoint, make and constitute my executors of this my present testament, that they may dispose for the health of my soul just as they shall answer in the presence of God [*coram summo Judice*] on the day of judgement. With these witnesses John Hed, John Sybryght, William Bungay and John Byrd.

[Proved at London, 12th Sept. 1486]

---

[1]   The friary of Babwell lay about ½ mile north of the north gate of Bury St Edmunds.

---

the Steeple [tower] of the said church of Lavenham for discharging of my conscience and my brother William Causton's conscience £40, the which £40 I was judged to pay to Lavenham Church by Master Thomas Stockhouse . . .[25].

From 1485 to 1540, when such bequests virtually ceased, a total of £2,287 was left specifically for the fabric of the church and its rebuilding by fifty donors or their executors. Of the donors at least thirty-five are known to have been involved in the cloth industry. This itself was a prodigious sum at a time when, for example, a labourer would be lucky to earn more than 6d a week, yet the total cost of the project must have been far greater (see Appendix 2). As well as the bequests in wills, other sums must have been raised locally, to which

quite ordinary folk would have had the chance of contributing. At the town of Eye in north Suffolk, for example, several methods of raising money were adopted for rebuilding the church tower in the late fifteenth century: by the holding of social events known as "church ales", by hiring out a plough used in the celebration of Plough Monday, but chiefly "by the franke and devoute hartes of the people" who gave what they could afford[26]. In all probability the situation at Lavenham was similar, and it would be wiser therefore to think of the church as the achievement of the whole parish, the poor as well as the rich, the anonymous as well as the documented[27].

Unfortunately we know very little about the people who actually planned and carried out the rebuilding. It is almost certain that John

Roger, a freemason mentioned in 1522, was engaged on the work. Perhaps the same is true of Robert King, a painter, and of William Galaunte and John Grace, both tilers (that is, brickmakers)[28]. Certainly much of the interior would have been painted, and a lot of brick was used on the inside of the great tower. It has been suggested that the masons of the abbey at Bury St Edmunds might have taken an active interest in the rebuilding. Simon Clerk was the resident master mason of Bury Abbey between 1445 and 1485, and also worked at Eton and on King's College Chapel in Cambridge. Clerk and his associate John Wastell signed contracts with the churchwardens of Great St Mary's, Cambridge, and of Saffron Walden in Essex; Lavenham's arcades and clerestories bear a strong resemblance to both those churches. Wastell was also resident in Bury; between 1485 and 1515 he succeeded Clerk at King's College and worked in the eastern counties. Associated with Wastell was Henry Seamark, who was working locally between 1482 and 1534. It is quite possible that one or more of these masons had a hand in Lavenham's design[29].

Some bequests in local wills refer to specific parts of the church during its rebuilding: tower,

Above right: *The impression or "indent" of a brass which marked the graves of Thomas Spring III (died 1523) and of his second wife Alice (died 1538). The tomb and screen cost 100 marks (£66 13s 4d).*

Right: *The magnificent interior of the church, with its late-fifteenth-century nave and fourteenth-century chancel. The Spring parclose is just visible through the arches of the north arcade.*

WILL OF THOMAS SPRING III, 1523

[*Note:* with the exception of the first six words translated from Latin, the original spelling and capitalization have been retained. Punctuation and paragraphing have been introduced as an aid to the reader. Abbreviated words have been extended, except for units of money].

In the name of God Amen, The xiii[th] Day of June, in the yere of our Lord god M[I] v[c] xxiii And in the xv yere of the Reigne of king Henry the viii[th], I Thomas Spryng of Lavenham in the Countie of Suffolke and in the Dioces of Norwiche, Clothmaker, being of hole mynde and memory and parfite remembraunce, and verely knowing that there is no thing more sure or more certeyn to any Creature in this Wretched Worlde than deth, whiche every creature lyving Inevitably must suffer, And nothing more unsuer and uncerteyn than the dredfull houre therof, Fully disposaing and purposing my self by the marcy, grace and help of the most mercifull lord crist Jesus to be at all and every tyme and houre redy, doo make my last Will and testament in maner and fourme folowyng. First I adnull and Revoke all other willes and testamentes ever afore this day made and declared, And will that every of them shalbe of noo strength nor effect. Item, I bequeth my soule to Almighty God, to his blissed moder mary, and to all the holy company of hevyn. And my body to be buried in the Church of Lavenham, before the awter of Saint Kateryn where I will be made a Tombe with a parclose therabout, by the discrecion of myn executors.[1]

Item, I bequeth to the high awter of Lavenham for my tithes and offeringes necligently forgotten and not paide Cs. [*solidos* = shillings]. Item I will that satisfaccion and restitucion be made to every persone compleyning and Duely proving any Iniurye, wronge, extorcion, oppression, disceyte or any misbehaving or demeanying ageynst reason and conscience, by me to them doon in any Wise. Item, I will that Immediatly after my decesse in as hasty tyme as it may be conveniently doon there shalbe a thousand masses songen for the welth of my soule. Item, I geve and bequeth to every of the houses of Freres of Clare, Sudbury, Babwell,[2] two houses of Freres in Thetford and the Nonnes of Thetford to pray for my soule and all my benefactours soules, and to every of them xls. Item, I will that there be disposaed the xxx[th] Day after my decesse and departing owt of this worlde, one hundred poundes in all suche townes and parisshes as I have any landes and tenementes, that is to sey to have a masse with Dirige in every Church, and the money to be disposaed to the prestes, Clerkes and pour folkes to pray for my soule and all my benefactours soules. Item, I geve and bequeth to the fynysshing of the Stepull of Lavenham two hundred poundes. Item, I geve and bequeth to the reparacion of high wayes, to be disposaed where myn executours shall thynke most necessary aboute the Towne of Lavenham, C marcas [hereafter translated as 'marks'; a mark was worth 13s 4d].

Item, I bequeth and geve to Alice my Wife, all hir apparell with Juelles, and one thousand marks in money and penyworthes,[3] over and beside six hundred marks that she brought to me at the tyme of hir mariage, which vi[c] [600] marks I will be paide her over and beside the said thousand marks. Item, I will that all my plate, ornamentes and Implementes of housholde, as bedding, naprye, hanginges, brasse, pewter and all other hostilmentes of howse, be devided bitwene my wife and John Spryng my sonne by myn executo(r)s. Item, I geve and bequeth to Alice my Wife ii of my best horses and iii kyne, suche as she will chose. Item, I will that the woode in my yardes and my Corne and Malt upon the Solers be equally devided bitwene my wife and John my sonne, except suche as shalbe spent by myn executours aboute my entirement and other things touching the ministracion of my goodes.

Item, I geve and bequeth towardes the mariage of Briget Spryng, my yongest daughter, fyve hundred marks, to be delivered to her at the age of xvi yeres. And if it happen the said Briget to dye afore she come to the age of xvi yeres, then I will the said fyve hundred marks be devided equally bitwene my Childers Childern

belfry, aisles, vestry, arches and windows. We know, too, that in the years following his death in 1523 the executors of Thomas Spring III spent a further £847 on the south aisle, on the endowment and building of a chantry chapel founded in his memory, on a tomb and magnificent parclose costing 100 marks, and on the raising of the tower (see Appendix 1). This

then lyving. Item, I geve and bequeth to John Spryng myn oldest sonne two hundred poundes. Item, I geve to Fraunces his doughter one hundred marks. Item, I geve and bequeth to Robert Spryng my sonne two hundred poundes. Item, I geve to every of the Childers of Thomas Jermyn nowe lyving xx li. [*libras* = pounds]. And yf any of theym dye before the age of xvi yeres, then I will the part or partes of theym so departed or decessed be evenly devided amonge the others then lyving. Item, I geve and bequeth to every Childe of my doughter Rose Guybon, nowe lyving, xx li. And if any of them dye before the age of xvi yeres, then I will that the part or partes of them so departed or decessed be evenly devided amonges the other then lyvinge. Item, I will that myn executours doo paye unto my wifes doughter Alice May, When she shalbe of the age of xvi yeres, xxvi li. xiiis. iiiid. [£26 13s 4d], which I recovered for hir of Mayes executours. Item, I will that if Robert Newman and William Gooding of Bockyng doo not paye the said Alice May xl li. at the age of xvi yeres, that then myn executours shall sue a certeyn obligacion in which they be bounde to me. Item, I geve and bequeth to every of my godchildern iiii. iiiid. [3s 4d] Item, I will there be distributed amonge my houshold servauntes somoch money as shalbe thoughte necessarye by the discrecion of myn executours.

The Residue of all my goodes and Catalles not gevyn nor bequethed I geve it to the disposicion of myn executours, Whom I ordeyn and make Sir William Waldgrave, knyght, and Thomas Jermyn my sonne in lawe, desiring and requiryng theym in the Way of Charitie to ordre and dispose the same in Charitable dedes, as they shall thinke most expedient to the pleasur of god and for the welth of my soule.[4]

Item, my mynde and will is that if my wife or any of my childern doo interupt, lett or troble any article comprysed in this my last wille and testament, soo that this my last wille cannot take effect according to the true entent thereof, Then I will that all legacies and bequests to them before gevyn that so do interupt, be voide and of noon effect, And that such person or persones so interupted or troubled shall have and enioye the same Legacye and bequest which was bequethed to him or them that shal make suche trouble, vexacion and besynes [business]. And further I require and charge John Springe myn oldest sonne, upon my blissinge, that he hynder not, distourbe nor lett this my testament and last will in noo poynt, But that he endevour himself as moch as in him is, to perfourme and accomplishe the same according to the trowth.

Item, I geve to the Bailif of Lavenham, William Betryn, one hundred poundes, whereof I will that John his sonne have xx li. Item, I geve and bequeth to Petir Gawge myn apprentice x half balys of woode [10 half balls of woad].

In witnesse of the trowth I have sealed and delivered this as my last wille and testament, In the presence of William Betryn, Bayly of Lavenham, Henry Symond, William Wooder and Petir Turnour.

[Proved at St Paul's, London, 3rd July 1523]

---

1 Thomas III was buried, as he requested, before the altar of St Katherine at the east end of the north aisle. Inside the elaborately carved wooden parclose his grave-stone can still be seen, carrying the impression of an elaborate double brass. Because a chantry chapel for the Braunche family had already (c. 1500) been built on the north side of the chancel, Spring's executors were forced to construct his chantry on the south—on the opposite side from his grave.

2 The friary of Babwell lay about ½ mile north of the north gate of Bury St Edmunds.

3 The phrase 'in pennyworths' appears to mean 'in kind'.

4 A detailed comparison of this document with the executors' accounts (Appendix 1) will show how the executors did indeed use their discretion, by disposing of large sums of money not mentioned in the will.

was over and above the £200 bequeathed to the tower in his will. Yet nothing is known about the detailed organization of the work. Compared with Walberswick, for example, which has its masons' contract and churchwardens' accounts, Lavenham church is not well documented for the most important period of its history.

Maintaining the highways

It has already been noted that sums bequeathed to the upkeep of highways also rose steeply in the early Tudor period, and again they prove largely to have been lavish bequests from wealthy clothiers. Before the Highway Act of 1555 these were a recognized expression of pious charity, and the gifts were indeed impressive. But it was also in the clothiers' best interests to maintain roads which must have carried considerable traffic in wool from Norfolk, Lincolnshire or the Midlands, as well as in rolls of finished cloth on their way to London, either directly by the "Clothing Road" through Essex or *via* the port of Ipswich.

The value and incidence of these bequests show that the roads around Lavenham were then regularly maintained, with the possible exception of "the foul way between Lavenham and Melford", for the repair of which the clothier William Sturmyn left five marks in 1493. All the main routes from Lavenham are mentioned, including the roads to Bury, Sudbury, Long Melford, Brent Eleigh, Boxford, Groton and Cockfield, as well as the streets in the town itself—an indication of the traffic generated by this busy industrial centre. In 1469 John Fermer, an aulnage collector of some importance, wanted "the highway opposite my house in Lavenham [to] be completely made up with sand beginning at my renter [house rented out] and proceeding to the north end of the street".

Before 1485 we find seventeen wills leaving money totalling £96 6s 8d for this purpose—an impressive average of £5 13s 4d per person. Yet between 1485 and 1540, eighteen wills left money for highway repair totalling £456 3s 4d—an average of over £25 per person and a quite remarkable figure for the period (see Appendix 4). Most of these donors were clothiers or widows of clothiers.

Right: *The handsome Angel Inn in the Market Place contains some fine early moulded and plastered ceilings. In 1529 it was owned by Thomas Sexton.*

Opposite page: *A considerable number of people have gathered round the Swan Hotel, perhaps for the start of a hunt, in this late-nineteenth-century scene.*

Streets and houses

Excluding housing estates built since the First World War, all the present principal streets of Lavenham, plus a few lost lanes, existed by the fifteenth century, and probably very much earlier. Wills reveal that some, like High Street, Prentice Street and Market Lane, have retained the same name, while others, like Barn Street and Lady Street, have changed theirs several times. Often the streets were named after principal inhabitants: for example, Grigges Street, Lynches Street, Bolton Street and Shilling Street.

Most of the clothiers of any stature owned a number of properties in the town, and it is not always possible to discover in which street they had their "headhouse". To be able to identify this house with a structure surviving today is even more rare. In 1529 Thomas Sexton owned the Angel in the Market Place and lived at the top of Church Street next to the tenter-yards adjoining the church. In 1539 Robert Critofte the elder owned the tenement in Prentice Street called "Sheltons . . . as it butteth upon Trinity Hall on one side and upon John Hunt on the other". Any building to the west of Trinity Hall would almost certainly have formed part of the Angel, so we may plot Critofte's tenement immediately to the east of

the hall, with John Hunt's next again—though Critofte had his looms and workshop, and probably lived, elsewhere in Prentice Street[30]. In Elizabethan times Roger Ruggles almost certainly lived in the house in Water Street now called The Priory, while Roger Grome occupied the The Willows or its predecessor.

The Causton family, clothiers, farmers, butchers and later scholars and schoolmasters, apparently lived in what is now called Little Hall and owned adjoining property. Symond Causton, in 1521, left to his son William his headhouse (after his mother's death) and the tenement next to it. William, in 1552, was "dwelling by the Cross in Lavenham", and Thomas, in 1624, refers to his headhouse as being "in or near Prentice Street". These descriptions seem to relate quite satisfactorily to Little Hall, which dates from the fourteenth and fifteenth centuries, and to the adjoining property on the corner of the Market Place and Prentice Street[31].

John Whatlock, a prosperous clothier and another owner of the Angel, was in 1556 almost certainly living in the house at the bottom of Lady Street which is now Nos 6 and 7. In his will he left "to John Whatlock my son my house, that I now dwell in in Barbours Street [Lady Street] with the new parlour . . . and my tenement on my backside abutting

17

Above: *Little Hall, which dates mainly from the fourteenth and fifteenth centuries, is now the headquarters of the Suffolk Preservation Society.*

Left: *The same house, subdivided into six cottages, before its restoration was begun by the Gayer-Anderson brothers in 1924. Its medieval character was then heavily concealed.*

Opposite page: *The same house in close-up today. Since 1924 the overhanging jetties have been restored and a double door of medieval type installed.*

upon Hockerells Street [Barn Street]". No 7 is a medieval house originally with an open hall, while No 6 is obviously the rebuilt parlour end[32].

John Newton, who appears to have been an agent or steward to the Earl of Oxford, left "unto Robarte Cooke the Elder of Lavenham shoemaker and Elizabeth his wife . . . my place called the Swanne and all my pasture called the Buttfelde". That was in 1544, but the Swan Hotel, well known to all who have visited Lavenham, was already venerable when Newton had it[33].

Many of Lavenham's remarkably abundant timber-framed buildings, all listed for preservation, are of high quality; they are the "executive" properties of their day. In the main they are characterized by a generous use of timber, often moulded and sometimes richly carved, by long overhangs ("jetties") and by the close spacing of studs. Architectural analysis and restoration have revealed many examples of medieval houses, where open halls have later been subdivided and ceiled[34]. There seems to have been no great pressure on building space, for unlike the houses in many larger towns which are at right angles to streets, Lavenham's lie parallel with them. Impressive as is the display of so many timber frames, many more lie hidden behind Georgian, Victorian and even later façades[35].

Occasionally a door at first-floor level, facing the street, is evidence of a former storeroom above living or working accommodation, where wool, yarn, cloth and agricultural produce were probably kept. Originally such doors are likely to have had hoists above them, like so many houses in Amsterdam today. Some ground-floor entrances are furnished with very large arched doors, presumably for the passage of goods, into which are fitted small, independently opening, personal doors; an excellent example can be seen at Molet House in Barn Street. Some plastered exteriors bear pargeted designs or emblems such as the mitre of Bishop Blaise, the patron saint of woolcombers, and the fleur-de-lys, which has also been associated with the cloth trade.

Tudor shop-fronts survive in Lady Street and in the Market Place to the east of the Guildhall[36].

Among frequent mentions of the Market Place are many bequests of stalls, either for unspecified trades or known to belong to butchers. One apparently permanent group of these, recurring in wills over a long period, was said to abut on the market tollhouse. The latter, therefore, seems to be the timber-framed cottage forming an island within the Market Place near the cross, or its predecessor on the same site[37]. The adjacent group of stalls became a butchers' "Shambles" and later a row of humble cottages strung across the Market Place in front of the Guildhall. The lane between them and the Guildhall range was known significantly as Butcher's Lane or the

Butchery. The cottages were not demolished until 1938.

The rich clothier William Jacob appears to have lived near the market, perhaps in Molet House in Barn Street. In his will of 1500 he directed that "a cross made at my proper cost be set on the Market Hill in Lavenham, the pattern to be the cross standing in Cambridge Market Place". The stepped base of Lavenham's cross, with a later shaft, is still there, but the "pattern" referred to in Cambridge has not survived for comparison[38].

The gilds

The pre-Reformation wills of Lavenham contain many bequests to local gilds. Four such fraternities or "clubs" existed in the town, dedicated to the Holy Trinity, Our Lady, Corpus Christi and SS Peter and Paul (usually referred to as St Peter's). In spite of what many local people and writers have said[38], their purpose was not to organize individual trades or crafts; they existed for religious and social reasons, and to give certain personal benefits to their members, who could be drawn from many different occupations.

At Bardwell in north Suffolk, a village with a population of about 600, the memoranda and accounts of an early-sixteenth-century gild happen to survive and enable us to see in some detail how it was run[40]. Needy members were helped from the funds, funeral rites were observed and masses said for the souls of departed members, candles were provided in the parish church before the Easter sepulchre and holy sacrament, and religious processions were organized on appropriate days. Occasional feasts were held, with other entertainments, so gildhalls needed to be fairly commodious, with facilities for cooking and feasting on a large scale (an official cook and a minstrel were regularly elected at Bardwell), and for the storage of food, drink and the gild's pewter, cutlery, furniture and valuables. At Bardwell the membership of a single gild numbered well over a hundred and included men and women, married and single; an alderman or president, various officers and a chaplain were elected annually.

Two of Lavenham's medieval gildhalls survive. That of Corpus Christi is the sumptuous and well-known building in the Market Place, while Our Lady's gildhall later became the Wool Hall in Lady Street, now part of the Swan Hotel. St Peter's gildhall was in the High Street, and Holy Trinity's occupied a site at the top of Prentice Street which is now a car park. These last two halls were demolished in 1896 and 1879 respectively, but old photographs of both are preserved. It is worth noting that

bequests were made to the gild of Corpus Christi well before the fifteen-twenties when the present "Guildhall" was supposedly erected, so there probably existed an earlier building, on the same site or elsewhere[41].

Naturally, the bequests made by members to their gilds varied in size and kind (see Appendix 3). For example, in 1416 John Carpenter

Opposite page: *The Market Cross before 1924. Of the cross given to the town by William Jacob c1500, only the stepped base survives; the present shaft bears the date 1725.*

Left: *An undated photograph shows another good example of the unselfconscious down-at-heel air of Lavenham as it was early this century.*

Below: *The same building today, significantly used as a tourist information centre. The sixteenth-century windows were originally unglazed; thus when the shop was open the two bottom shutters were propped to form a counter and the upper pair were chained up to the jetty.*

left the sum of 40 shillings to the gild of the Holy Trinity while another member, Elizabeth Braunche, left a piece of property in 1501. William Schedde, in 1469, wanted the aldermen of Trinity gild to have the gift and disposition of six houses for the poor for ever. In 1473 John Harry left a sum of money to the same gild, specifically to support a chaplain who would say masses for the souls of its

Left: *The Gildhall of the Holy Trinity in Prentice Street. This medieval building, which had been given a major Georgian remodelling, was demolished in 1879.*

Opposite page: *The demolition of the Gildhall of Saints Peter and Paul in High Street in 1896. Since the dissolution of the gild this building had been used as a wool store and latterly as a storehouse for Ropers' mat factory, as seen on page 89.*

Below: *The Gildhall of Our Lady in Lady Street. One of two medieval gildhalls to survive in Lavenham today, this is now part of the Swan Hotel.*

brethren "time without end". Edmund Bownde, a member of St Peter's gild, left in 1504 some of his best tableware, "my great mazer [bowl], twelve pieces of pewter and a tablecloth", and Roger Trype in 1526 left money expressly for the upkeep of St Peter's gildhall and its barn[42].

By Acts of Parliament in 1545 and 1547, all religious and social gilds were abolished (whereas trade gilds in large towns were not affected). Their property was confiscated by the Crown, and often sold off or granted to private individuals at a later date. It is recorded, for example, that on 16th December, 1548, John Earl of Oxford and Thomas Almotte, gentleman, were granted various lands which had belonged to the "late" gild of SS Peter and Paul of Lavenham[43]. This so-called reform suddenly destroyed ancient and valued institutions which had for generations given ordinary men and women the warmth of comradeship and a measure of personal security. For a time, at any rate, the quality of social and communal life must have seriously declined.

Of course to some extent the gilds were elitist, in that their members tended to be the more prosperous representatives of local society, but hundreds of these fraternities existed in Suffolk alone, and they must have had thousands of members. The real cause of their downfall was the inextricable association with late-medieval religion. They were viewed by Protestant reformers as idolatrous and superstitious, not without justification. For instance, a Lavenham clothier named John Rysby had applied, a few weeks before his death in 1493, to become a member of St Peter's gild. In the presence of his own chaplain, of the gild's priest and some of the brethren, he promised 6s 8d to the gild, and in return asked "to become a brother" and "to be partaker of their prayers". Clearly he sought the benefits of a gild funeral, and in particular the prayers and masses which would help to save his soul from the torments of purgatory[44].

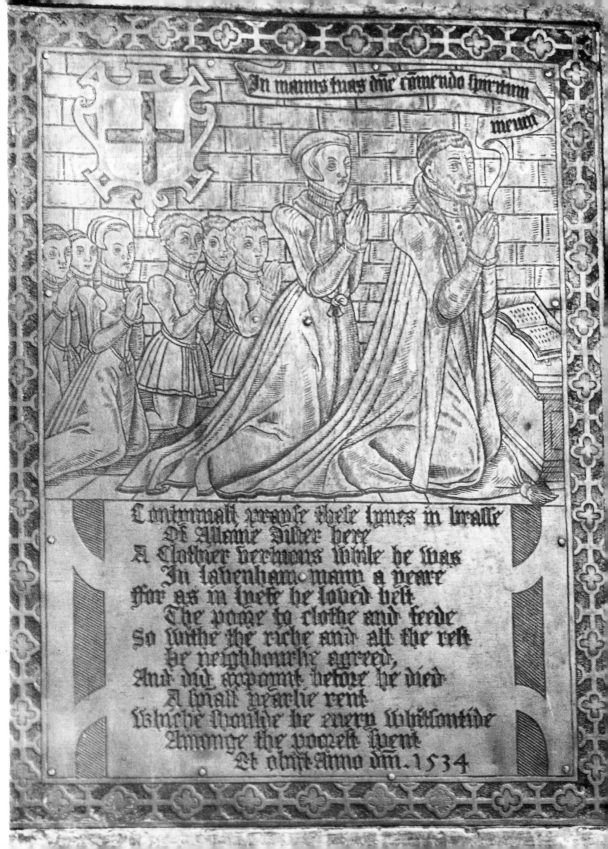

In manus tuas dñe comendo spiritum meum

Continuall prayse these lynes in brasse
Of Allenne Dister here
A Clothier vertuous while he was
In lavenham many a yeare
for as in liefe he loved best
The poore to clothe and feede
So with the riche and all the rest
he neighbourlie agreed,
And did appoynt before he died
A speciall yearlie rent
Which shoulde be every Whitsontide
Amonge the poorest spent
Et obiit Anno dñi 1534

Left: *The brass of Allaine Dister in the north aisle of Lavenham Church. Many Lavenham brasses were destroyed after the Reformation, so this is a rare depiction of a local clothier involved with the Old Draperies. He died in 1534, and is here described as charitable and "a clothier vertuous".*

Below: *A Tudor cloth weaver at his loom.*

The Making of Broadcloth 2

LAVENHAM had a remarkable concentration of people who called themselves "clothiers" or "clothmakers". They ranged from very large employers, who were often considerable merchants as well, to others who were barely distinguishable from ordinary craftsmen such as master-weavers. The essential characteristic of clothiers was that they organized and financed large sections of the industry; they provided the capital or credit to buy the raw wool, recruited and paid various craftspeople, and also organized the sale and dispatch of finished cloth. The range of business interests possessed by a rich clothier is neatly summarized by the title given to Thomas Spring III in 1508: he was described as "clothmaker", "yoman" and "merchaunt"[45].

Much of the business of making and selling cloth was clearly conducted on credit. Many clothiers' wills refer to debts owing to them and by them. For example, in 1544 John Barker, clothmaker of Lavenham, reminded his executors that his namesake John Barker of Bildeston "do owe me three score 5 pounds 15 shillings for certain broadcloths that he had of mine"[46]. Thomas Spring III, the "Rich Clothier" of Lavenham, when assessed in 1522, was reckoned to be owed as much as £2,200 in debts, both "sperate and desperate"[47]. On the other hand, yet another John Barker, clothier of Lavenham, died in 1609 owing a London grocer £90 8s 0d[48]. Payment was also made in kind, as is well revealed in the ledger of Thomas Howell, a draper of London; he dealt with many clothiers in Suffolk and Essex, and

in return for their cloth forwarded not only sums of money but raw materials such as woad and oil[49]. The granting of credit remained important to men of business after the old industry or Old Draperies had died out. For example John Pinchbeck, senior, who had a draper's shop in Lavenham's High Street, left houses and lands to his four sons in 1648, "but in consideration of one hundred and odd pounds which I owe, besides what I owe for shop wares, and knowing that my shop will do no more than pay my debts which I owe for shop wares"[50].

The control exercised by clothiers over the whole industry is well demonstrated by the equipment and stocks of materials which they bequeathed. In 1498 Thomas Braunche wanted his nephew to stay with his widow, "being unto her good, gentle, true and serviceable until

Blackwell Hall, the great cloth market in the City of London, as shown on Ralph Agas' plan of 1560–70. The arrow marks its site adjacent to the Guildhall.

such wool and stuff belonging thereto in my house will be wrought out"[51]. Many others left stocks of wool, yarn, dyeing materials, looms and, of course, cloth.

References to the purchase of wool are rare. Certainly some locally-grown wool, for example from the Breckland and parts of High Suffolk, found its way into the manufacturing districts[52]. In 1419 Adam Skynnere of Lavenham bought thirty wool-fells for 6s 0½d from the steward of Dame Alice de Bryene who lived at nearby Acton[53], but East Anglian wool was not rated highly[54] and local manufacturers certainly drew on other areas such as Lincolnshire, Northamptonshire, Buckinghamshire and Leicestershire[55]. For example, Roger Reve of Bury St Edmunds referred in his will of 1538 to "six packs of my Lyncolnshire wolle"[56].

Although some of the finished cloth was sold locally and in other parts of England, most of it was probably exported overseas. Cloth destined for export was sent through the market at Blackwell Hall in London, and found its way to "Eastland [Baltic countries], Russia, Spain, Barbary [North Africa], France and Turkey and other places"[57]. The Merchant Adventurers and members of the Mercers' Company of London were particularly prominent in the wholesale exporting of woollen cloth. Their main outlets were in Flanders and the Low Countries, especially through the four great seasonal fairs at Bruges, Bergen-op-Zoom, Antwerp and Middelberg. The wills of John

Hunte (1539) and Robert Grome (1540), both of Lavenham, refer to debts owing to them "as well beyond the sea as on this side". When John Grome died in 1587 he left 30s to be distributed among the poor of Lavenham "within six months of the return of Thomas Grome my brother from Venice"[58]. These comments give us a fleeting glimpse of the far-flung contacts which must have been commonplace among the richer clothiers and merchants of Lavenham. The remarkable ledger of Thomas Kytson, merchant of London and squire of Hengrave, shows how shiploads of cloth and other goods were organized and sent to the Low Countries[59].

However capitalist and highly organized the cloth industry was, and whatever its overall scale, it remained essentially domestic, with craftsmen, including women and children, working mainly in their own homes. They took in carefully weighed and recorded materials, which remained the property of the clothier. The only exceptions to this pattern were processes which demanded heavier and costlier equipment, or special sites: a good example is dyeing, with its vats, hearths and vital water supply.

From an early date, certainly by the end of the fifteenth century, the tendency existed for craftsmen to be directly employed. They might have owned their own tools and equipment, such as spinning wheels and looms, but they were increasingly likely to be supplied with their raw materials (wool, yarn or webs of cloth) by clothiers who paid them wages piecemeal. Thus in 1486 Thomas Spring II bequeathed 100 marks to be distributed among his spinners, fullers and weavers, whom he had doubtless organized and paid (see p. 12). The spinners and weavers probably worked in their own homes, but the fullers and dyers may have worked at the clothier's head-house or other premises owned by him. By the early sixteenth century it is clear that the independent crafts-man, who not only owned his own gear but set his own prices and conditions, was fast disappearing.

While most of the employees lived in Lavenham and surrounding villages like Cockfield and Preston, others lived at a considerable distance. In 1493 Thomas Sturmyne bequeathed 2d to each of his spinners who lived at Glemsford and Stoke-by-Clare (the latter being some fifteen miles from Lavenham)[60]. In the seventeenth century a Lavenham clothier even had spinners in Cambridge[61]. A remarkable Elizabethan inventory from Stoke-by-Clare shows in considerable detail the web of employment which

A map showing the clothing towns of west Suffolk and north Essex.

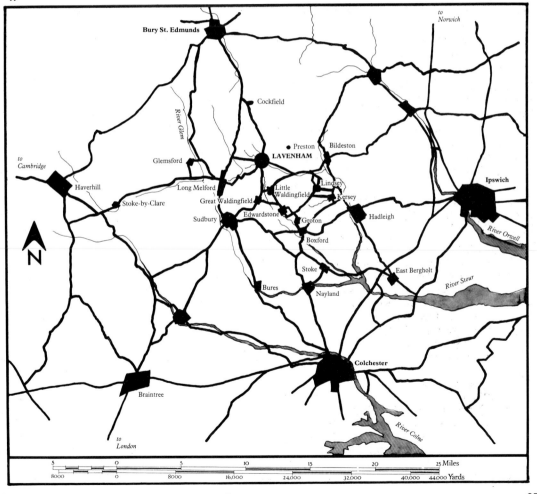

centred on a clothier (and a relatively poor one, at that): Thomas Reynoldes at his death in 1576 owed debts to a London man for oil; to four men, two of whom lived at Chilton by Clare, for "Dressynge of clothe"; to four men, whose places of residence are not specified, for "wevynge of clothe"; to one man of Clare for "dying of lyste & Wolle"; to three men for "thyckynge of clothe", two of whom lived at Clare and the third at Sawston in Cambridgeshire; and to three married women and a widow, of unknown parishes, for "spynnynge of Wolle".

Spinners

In the Lavenham area the spinning of yarn was a craft which lasted longer than weaving. It was primarily the work of women and children; no doubt they were poorly paid, but the work brought in a useful and sometimes vital contribution to the family's income. Wool was normally delivered to a spinner by weight, and when she returned it in the form of yarn it was again weighed. Before it could be spun, however, the raw wool had to be carded using pairs of wool cards which resembled wire

---

INVENTORY OF THOMAS REYNOLDES OF STOKE BY CLARE, 1576

[Extract only] [SRO (B), IC500/3/1 (43)]

dettes owynge by the testator

Imprimis to mr hattes of london for Oyle		xx^s	
Item to Father Collyn' of Chylton & to hys sone for dressynge of clothe		xxix^s	iiii^d

Imprimis to mr hattes of london for Oyle — xx^s

Item to Father Collyn' of Chylton & to hys sone for
    dressynge of clothe — xxix^s iiii^d
        to Gyles Banbrygge & Gregorye Sherman for dressynge
            of Clothe — xxiii^s vi^d
        to Wylliam Crosall & Nycolas Martyn for Wevynge of
            Clothe — xviii^s iiii^d
        to Michell Sexton & Borham for Wevynge of Clothe — vi^s ii^d
        to Ive of Clare for dyinge of lyste & Wolle — iii^s vi^d
        to Henry Ive of Sawston for thyckynge of Clothe — iii^s iiii^d
        to mr Danvers of Clare for thyckynge of Clothe — xx^d
        to mr Wylson of Clare for thyckynge of Clothe — xv^d
        to John Twyddes Wyeff for spynnynge of Wolle — iii^s ix^d
        to Roger Huryelles Wyeff for spynnynge of Wolle — iii^s x^d
        to Clement Algers Wyeff for spynnynge of Wolle — iii^s x^d
        to the Wydowe Jannynge for spynnynge of Wolle — ii^s viii^d
        to Thomas Strondes Wyeff for spynnynge of Wolle — ii^s
        to the Goodman Rewse — xx^s
        to George Reynoldes hys sone — xl^s
        to James Reynoldes hys sone — iiii^li iii^s iiii^d
        to John Bredge — xvii^s
        to John Wade — iiii^s
        to Reynold Dyke — ii^s
        to Thomas Porter — iiii^s vii^d
        to John Cropley ii^s iiii^d to Richard kynge xii^d — iii^s iiii^d
        to John Crysall of Clare — ii^s i^d

Summa xiiii^li xix^s ii^d
[Total £14 19s 2d]

The lady depicted on this medieval misericord in Norton Church, Suffolk, is smoothing out woollen fibres by means of cards, in preparation for spinning yarn.

brushes. Matted locks of raw wool were repeatedly brushed between the cards, teasing out the fibres, reversing root to tip and tip to root until a smooth, aerated and perfect mix resulted. The whole craft is usefully described in a petition from Suffolk clothiers in 1575 (key words are italicized): "the custom of our country is to carry *our* wool out to carding and spinning and *put it to* divers and sundry spinners who have *in their houses* divers and sundry children and servants that do card and spin the said wool"[62].

Although spinning set large numbers of people to work, it did not necessarily give steady employment but was liable to fluctuations of boom and slump. For example, changes in foreign policy affected the markets used by English traders, and a fall in demand for cloth overseas could soon make itself felt in the spinning districts. During the depression of 1623, a further complication arose in Babergh Hundred: churchwardens and overseers were required to deal with the complaint that well-off farmers' wives, children and servants were getting most of the spinning work, and excluding more needy families. The overseers were to go to the "packhouses" and persuade clothiers to "put out their spinning work unto the poorer sort . . . and desire those that be wives of farmers or yeomen that they will forbear to seek to get any of the said work from the poor that have no other means to live by . . ."[63].

The traditional form of spinning in medieval and earlier times had been by distaff (or "rock") and spindle and, incredible though it may seem, it still lingered on in rural East Anglia until the early nineteenth century[64]. However, two inventions speeded up the process. The first was the "great wheel" or large flywheel set in motion by hand, which was introduced into England probably before the fourteenth century. The second was the standard spinning-wheel turned by pedal, which appeared around the middle of the sixteenth century. These two mechanical innovations, foreshadowing in a minor way the effect of the spinning jenny and mule on the eighteenth-century cotton industry, may have stimulated the English cloth industry during the fifteenth and sixteenth centuries by producing larger quantities of cheaper yarn for weavers to work on. Local references to spinning-wheels do not, however, distinguish the types involved at this period.

Weavers

Weavers, on the whole, must originally have worked as independent craftsmen, able to negotiate their own terms. At one end of the scale, the more prosperous weavers became clothiers; the rest, however, sank to the level of wage-earners. In 1539 the weavers of Lavenham, with those of Ipswich, Hadleigh and Bergholt, petitioned against the restrictive practices of clothiers. They complained that

weaving is the central process of the industry, weavers gradually fell into economic subjection, and only three in Lavenham were substantial enough to leave wills.

The looms and stocks of materials, when they are mentioned in wills, are commonly disposed "in the shop" (that is, workshop) which was part of the deceased person's house. No evidence exists for purpose-built, large-scale premises of the kind described by Thomas Deloney (1543–1600) in his poem

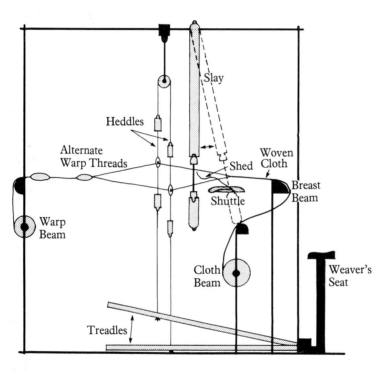

Left: *A simplified diagram to explain the principle of the traditional loom, whose design remained basically unchanged throughout the whole period of clothmaking in Lavenham.*

Right: *In 1609 a royal charter set up a short-lived incorporation of clothiers, woollen workers and tailors in Bury St Edmunds and western Suffolk. This extract deals with the suppression of abuses in the trade. [SRO(B): D9/1/1a]*

clothiers were keeping looms, weavers and fullers in their own houses, with the result that independent weavers were gradually impoverished. "For the rich men, the clothiers, be concluded and agreed among themselves to hold and pay one price for weaving, which price is too little to sustain households upon, working day and night, holy day and week day, and many weavers are therefore reduced to the position of servants"[65]. In spite of the fact that

about the famous John Winchcombe or Jack of Newbury. That west-country clothier is said to have possessed 200 looms working in one "large, long room"[66]. Although it is possible that outhouses served as weaving sheds, wills never mention more than a small number of looms, which could be accommodated in any fair-sized room. Some of Lavenham's ancient houses have sockets in their structural timbers that may have housed frames and pegs on which warp was wound, but looms themselves, because they were free-standing, appear to have left no traces. It is interesting that among the ordinances drawn up in 1477 between the weavers of Bury St Edmunds and the bailiffs of the abbot, for the better control of the craft, is a decree prohibiting a weaver from having more than four looms at any one time[67]. This was in a tightly controlled industrial town with trade gilds; a smaller town like Lavenham would have had fewer restrictions. Even so,

the number of looms owned by individuals was always small.

In 1440 John Bolton, whose family gave its name to one of Lavenham's streets, left his son Thomas "a pair of [his] worse looms" and his son John "a pair of [his] best looms"[68]. A "pair" in fact meant only one implement made of separate parts, as we refer today to pairs of scissors or trousers. The solid wooden frames were, no doubt, well within the competence of local carpenters to erect. The other main parts

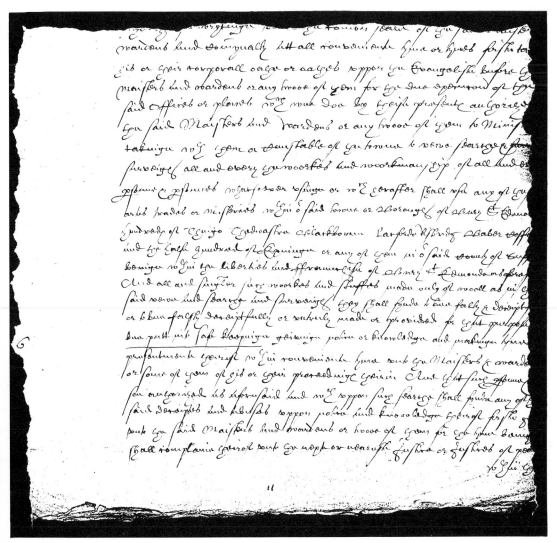

of a traditional loom were the beams, rollers or "trendles" on which yarn and cloth were wound; treadles for the feet connected to "heddles" which raised or lowered the warp to form the passage or "shed" through which the shuttle was thrown; and the hinged frame or "slay" which compacted the weave and contained reeds dividing the warp.

Left: *A weaver at work, from Jost Amman and Hans Sachs,* The Book of Trades, *1568.*

Opposite page: *A dyer at work, from the same source. Notice the tenter frame in the background for drying and stretching cloth.*

Below: *At the bottom of Prentice Street, with its abundant front steps, runs the River Brett. The clean break between town and country still fortunately survives. Notice the house on the left, divided into three tenements, each guarded by a wary mother.*

Dyers and dyehouses

The tradition that Lavenham's famous blue cloth was "dyed in the wool" (that is, before being woven) is substantiated by the specific mention of stocks of blue wool in at least six Lavenham wills from 1440 onwards. As late as 1592 Roger Ruggles of Water Street, Lavenham, was charged with having dyed a large quantity of wool with logwood, a blue dye regarded as inferior and forbidden by law[69]. The approved dye was prepared from the woad plant, which for centuries appears to have been imported from overseas, mainly from Toulouse in south-western France. In the early sixteenth century Robert Daundy, a merchant of Ipswich, sold woad and other commodities to Thomas Sexten, a leading Tudor clothier of Lavenham[70]. From the seventeenth century onwards woad was grown in various parts of England, principally Lincolnshire and Somerset.

The leaves of the plant were crushed and dried in the form of balls which were frequently mentioned in local wills. For example, Peter Gauge, an apprentice of Thomas Spring III, was left ten half-balls of woad when his master died in 1523[71]. The executors' accounts reveal that a full ball of woad was then worth more than £3. Dyers had to crumble this material and soak it so that it fermented to produce a clay-like substance which could then be put into the dyeing vats. Another closely related vegetable dye which made its appearance in England in the early seventeenth century was indigo; in 1609 John Barker, a clothmaker of Lavenham, owed £90 8s 0d to one Eldred, a London grocer, for 271 lb of "indico", which at 6s 8d a pound was another expensive commodity[72]. Such costly imports were often paid for out of moneys owing from abroad for the sale of cloth. Alum was another vital raw material, used by dyers as a fixer of colours or mordant; this is mentioned in William Spryng's inventory of 1476, together with bay-salt and oil[73].

Different shades of blue were obtained by

varying the concentration of dye. For example, the same amount of woad would dye three "blews" or six "azures" or twelve "plunketts"[74]. It should also be noted that some wills mentioned stocks of red wool, and that a Lavenham man forfeited red cloth for a technical offence in 1434–35[75]. In 1520 John Ponder left his wife "all my woad . . . and all the grene"; the latter referred not to the colour green but to "grain" which was an extremely expensive scarlet dye made from the body of an insect living on one species of Mediterranean oak[76]. A more economic red dye was madder, which was grown in the fourteenth century at nearby Great Waldingfield, and for which the city of Norwich had a special market[77]. In the district around Lavenham, cloths of many other colours are mentioned including murrey, peuce (a bluish black), russet, musterdevillers (a mixed grey) and popingay green[78].

Exactly how dyeing was organized in late medieval times is difficult to establish, but two

Elizabethan wills offer useful clues. In 1562 Roger Grome left to his son "my headhouse wherein I now dwell with the dyehouse, leads [leaden vessels], cisterns and woad-vats to the same belonging". Roger Grome's house was probably the now-Georgian-fronted house in High Street known as The Willows. A stream flowing through its garden feeds a canal or reservoir and then flows into a large cistern known to be of ancient origin and now covered by the bus shelter. William Grome, senior, in 1553 had bequeathed his house in the High Street "nighe the sesterne". Here the dyehouse was obviously adjacent to the clothier's house, but this was not always the case. In 1580 Roger Ruggles, who lived in Water Street, bequeathed "my dyehouse with the backside as it lieth together to the same dyehouse with the watercourse there" and also "one house which I bought of Roger Grome in the High Street with a copper and three vats and all other things belonging to a dyehouse"[79]. We may at least conclude that the essentials for dyeing were a suitable building, leads, cisterns, vats, coppers, hearths for heating water and a watercourse. Lavenham, in fact, has a remarkable system of brick-built culverts under some of its main streets[80]: one of their main purposes may have been to supply water to, and remove effluent from, the workplaces of dyers and fullers. The archaeological excavation of a local dyehouse, if it were possible, could provide new and valuable detail about the processes and materials involved.

We cannot prove the exact location of the dyehouses in Lavenham, although in neighbouring Long Melford the sites of some dyehouses are known from a map of 1580[81]. Nevertheless it is highly likely that Roger Ruggles' two dyehouses were both beside a tributary of the River Brett which runs through the centre of the town. One site was Roger Grome's house mentioned above and the other was probably halfway down Water Street where the culverted stream fed yet another reservoir on its way to the River Brett. Several other dyehouses must have existed, for most of the big clothiers mentioned them, or shares in them, in their wills. In 1476 Roger Crytott bequeathed a dyehouse to each of his two sons; to one he left "the dyehouse to chercheward" and to the other "the dyhous onto Buryward sumetyme clepyd [called] Carpenters Dyhous". (The clothier John Carpenter, presumably the earlier owner of the second dyehouse, died as early as 1416[82].) Two other

The culvert under The Priory in Water Street. At an early date a natural stream flowing down this street was culverted; some of the existing brickwork is fifteenth-century.

streams feed the river on the Bury side of Lavenham, so all told the town was fairly well provided with suitable sites and watercourses, both natural and man made.

Wills often mention "my part" or "my share" of a dyehouse. Though other factors might be involved such as joint investment, the division of inheritances is certainly one explanation of this phenomenon. For example, Thomas Wyllymott, who died in 1460, left to his sons John and Robert, after his wife's death, "my part in the dyehouse as I have it, to them and their heirs forever". Presumably he had owned a half-share, for the son Robert when he died in 1502 left his wife Elizabeth "the fourth part of the dyehouse". In 1504 Elizabeth in her turn bequeathed this part to her son and daughter[83].

Some dyers were independent masters who worked for themselves and had the capital or credit necessary to equip themselves. Others, like "Great John the Dyer", were the employees of local clothiers[84].

Fullers and shearmen

Fulling, the process of scouring and thickening the woven cloth, involved steeping the cloth in water, to which was added fullers' earth (a clay-like substance) or urine to help remove the grease. Here in its trough the cloth was subjected to pounding. For centuries this was done simply by treading with the feet, which incidentally gave rise to the surnames Walker and Footer, but from the thirteenth century onwards the process was mechanized, water power being harnessed to operate heavy wooden mallets which pounded the cloth. Such fulling mills are mentioned in medieval manorial documents at Hadleigh, Clare, Flatford and many other locations in Suffolk[85]. After scouring and beating, the cloth had to be smoothed repeatedly until it reached its appointed width. Then it was washed in clear water to remove any trace of soapiness.

Where fulling was carried out in Lavenham is not precisely revealed in wills. In 1528 a

A shearman at work, from Jost Amman and Hans Sachs, The Book of Trades, *1568. This craftsman could shave cloth remarkably finely with his heavy iron shears.*

fuller named John Lymmour bequeathed to his son a house in Water Street "towards the common", which would have been well placed for a water supply, but we do not know if he carried on his business there. In 1538 Roger Grome of Lavenham left "all the instruments belonging to my occupation called fuller's craft" to his son John, but no mention is made of the location of their tenement[86]. A water mill undoubtedly existed to the north of the town, but it is not known whether it was ever adapted to fulling. (Bourne Mill at Colchester is a water mill which originally ground corn but was subsequently given fulling stocks or mallets[87].)

When fulled, the cloths were attached to frames called tenters to be dried and stretched back to their true dimensions. Many tenter yards or tenter gardens were mentioned in wills, generally adjoining the owner's tenement and all bequeathed by clothiers. Thomas Sexton, a clothier whose will was made in 1529, left to his wife the house in which he dwelt "with the tenter yards between the house and Lavenham church"[88]. This block of land, immediately east of the church, is still called Tenter Piece. Conversely, none of the fullers' wills mention tenter yards. Considering the difficulty of handling and moving great lengths of wet cloth, one would have expected tenters to be adjacent to the fulling troughs, and it therefore seems likely that fullers went to work on the clothiers' premises.

When a house in Church Street was recently restored a wall supporting an inserted staircase was found to have been constructed from lengths of an old tenter frame. It still bore its tenter hooks, L-shaped nails subsequently driven flush with the surface of the timber[89]. Another similar example has come to light at The Priory[90].

Next, the cloth received the skilled atten-tions of a shearman. It was repeatedly wetted and brushed with teazles in order to raise and comb the nap; at first soft teazles were used, and then harder ones. In between the brush-ings and wettings the cloth was allowed to dry and shaved smooth, up to three times, with huge shears. The five wills of master shearmen from Lavenham are all dated between 1542 and 1615[91]. Perhaps before that time the shearmen did not have enough possessions to warrant the making of a will, and some of the smaller clothiers might have done the finishing work for themselves. John Browne certainly had his own business in 1542, for he left his son "half my tassell unstavid [unmounted teazles], six pairs of shears with all other implements and stuff belonging to my occupation within my [work]shop and without, he to pay and discharge all such duties as belongeth to my occupation". It is an interesting sidelight on this specialization that teazles were being grown in the Babergh area as a field crop in the early fourteenth century[92]. The fuller's distinc-tive teazle (*Dipsacus fullonem*) was the kind bearing hard hooked spines, not to be confused with the common field teazle with its straight spines.

Left: *Relatively modern tenter frames, supported by metal feet, at Otterburn mill, Northumberland, this century.*

Opposite page: *Fragments of tenter frame found at Lavenham. These timbers of unknown date had been reused in a building behind The Priory. Notice the L-shaped nails or "tenter hooks" which tensioned the cloth.*

Types of cloth

Aulnage accounts mention three main categories of cloth being made in Suffolk during the fifteenth century: broadcloths, narrow cloths or "dozens", and "streytes". An East Anglian broadcloth was required by a statute of 1467–68 to be 28 yards 28 inches long and 1¾ yards broad (5 feet 3 inches), and to be 38 lb in weight. A "streyte" was half the length of a broadcloth, half its width and a quarter of its weight; it was taxed therefore as a quarter of a broadcloth[93]. Parishes seem to have developed different emphases in their weaving: in 1466 Lavenham, Glemsford and Clare were taxed exclusively on broadcloth; the Waldingfields seem to have concentrated on narrow cloth, though they made some "streytes" as well; Hadleigh's large output consisted mainly of narrow cloths with smaller quantities of both "streytes" and broadcloth[94].

Aulnage accounts certainly do not reveal the full variety, because cheaper fabrics were excluded from taxation and from set standards. From an array of sources it is known that the following kinds of cloth were also made in Suffolk: "handywarps", which were very light, "kerseys", which were said in the fifteenth century to be 18 yards by 1 yard 1 inch (and which probably have no connection with the Suffolk village of Kersey, in spite of local belief), and undyed "whites" such as "Coxsall-whites" and "Glaynesfordes" (named after Coggeshall and Glemsford respectively)[95].

The different sizes and qualities of cloth can also be inferred from some local wills. When William Rysby, a clothier of Lavenham, died in 1506 he left to his wife not only "wool and woad and cloth to the full value of 100 marks, and the best pair of looms . . " but also "a wetcloth slay and a settcloth slay". He also left to his servant Simon Risby "my old loom . . . and a wetcloth slay and a settcloth slay"[96]. As has been mentioned, a slay is that part of a loom which divides the warp and compacts the weave. Clearly a single loom might have two or more slays for different weaves. Settcloth, sometimes called "vesses", was a light cheap cloth, free from official restrictions on stretching and not generally approved for export. Perhaps wetcloth by contrast was the best broadcloth, which was subject to every kind of inspection.

Lavenham's Heyday 3

FOR THE fifteen-twenties the evidence of wills is supplemented by two other remarkable documents, the Muster Roll or Military Survey of 1522, which happens to survive for the hundred of Babergh, and the Lay Subsidy of 1524 which is in print for the whole of Suffolk. In each case we are given a long list of names and other details which can be analysed to show how Lavenham compared with other places[97].

The Muster of 1522 gives the names of 157 heads of households in Lavenham, usually with a statement of their occupation and wealth (expressed in land, debts owing, moveables or wages). On the basis of their wealth people were required to provide arms for the muster or to serve at arms themselves. Thus Edmund Geffery, a smith by trade, had to provide two harnesses, one bow, one sheaf of arrows, one bill and a horse worth at least £1.

It is immediately noticeable that a third of all the occupations in the town were specifically concerned with the manufacture of cloth. There were thirty-three "clothmakers" or clothiers, who were the financiers and organizers of all the various processes, fourteen weavers, three fullers, three dyers and two shearmen. Furthermore it is highly likely that a fair proportion of the fifty-one labourers mentioned in the roll were involved in the cloth industry; the same might be true of the three mercers and two carriers. It is a reasonable guess that more than half of the total working population of the town were in various ways connected with clothmaking.

The proportion of clothiers is in itself remarkable—58% of all the people definitely involved in the industry. No other place in Babergh Hundred shows such a concentration; Glemsford was the nearest rival with twenty clothiers and Nayland next with fourteen, while Lavenham's immediate neighbour, Long Melford, had only eight, as did the large town of Sudbury. The same sort of irregularity can be seen in other occupations. Lavenham had fourteen weavers, the second highest total in the hundred but easily exceeded by Boxford with thirty-seven. It therefore looks as if Boxford, with no more than eleven clothiers, was a specialized weaving centre. Not surprisingly, the highest number of fullers was in parishes along the River Stour where a good water supply was available—at Melford nine, Bures six and Sudbury five. Bures, in fact, had only seven households directly connected with the making of cloth, of whom six were fullers. Similarly, by far the highest counts of shearmen, engaged in finishing cloth, were at Nayland (nine) and Boxford (six). From all these distributions the industry appears to have been organized over a fairly wide area within which individual parishes developed dominant, though not exclusive, specializations.

Another third of the working population of Lavenham in 1522 was concerned with retail trades, crafts and services which had nothing to do with cloth. As John Patten has shown, these were the occupations we would expect in an ordinary market town in Tudor times—six tailors, three bakers, two butchers, one miller,

The smithy in Water Street in the late nineteen-forties. The blacksmithing and welding business of Frederick Huffey and Sons reminds us of the range of traditional crafts and trades possessed by Lavenham for many centuries.

two barbers, three smiths, one chandler, one scrivener and one surgeon[98]. Only a collar-maker and shoemaker represented the leather trades, which were to become more important in the seventeenth century. Had it not been for the cloth industry, Lavenham would have been comparatively unremarkable, exceeded in economic standing by towns like Sudbury and Bury St Edmunds.

The Lay Subsidy of 1524 lists 195 heads of Lavenham households who paid tax to the crown that year. In the hundred of Babergh only Sudbury had more payers, with 218. The Muster Roll gave 157 names, of whom thirty-nine did not appear in the Lay Subsidy; of the Lay Subsidy's 195 names, seventy-seven did not appear on the Muster Roll. By conflating both lists, we get the names of some 240 heads of households who lived in Lavenham in the early fifteen-twenties—surely the vast majority. Only those who were very poor *and* disabled will have escaped mention. On the other hand, because the two sources are not strictly contemporary, a degree of over-recording must be acknowledged: some families present in 1522 would have left by 1524, and at this peak of Lavenham's fortune new immigrants would, in the meantime, have moved in. In spite of these reservations, and using the average size of households suggested by Peter Laslett (4.75), we may calculate that the total population of Lavenham in the early fifteen-twenties was probably around 1,100

OCCUPATIONS IN LAVENHAM, 1522

[from Military Survey of 1522, Suffolk Records Society, Vol. xxviii (1986)]

Occupation	No of individuals	Approximate classification
Clothmaker (that is, clothier)	33	Textiles
Weaver	14	
Dyer	3	
Fuller	3	
Shearman	2	
Mercer	3	
Carrier	2	Transport and equipment for horses
Smith	3	
Collar-maker	1	
Shoemaker	1	Makers of clothing
Tailor	6	
Tiler	2	Building
Freemason	1	
Painter	1	
Baker	3	Processors of food and retailers
Miller	1	
Butcher	2	
Chandler	1	
Scrivener	1	Services
Surgeon	1	
Barber	2	
Farmer	1	Agriculture
Yeoman	1	
Husbandman	2	
Labourer	51	Social groups rather than specific occupations
Servant	1	
Gentleman	1	
Widow	7	
Unspecified	7	
Lord of manor (non-resident)	1	
Steward	1	

souls[99]. Against national trends, the town had undoubtedly been growing in the fifteenth century. It can be no accident that among the people who migrated from the well-documented Huntingdonshire village of Warboys between 1400 and 1458 were three who came to live in Lavenham[100], and that in the same period at least two natives of the Low Countries were also given permission to live in the town[101].

W. G. Hoskins has shown from the subsidy returns of 1524 that Lavenham was then the

41

fourteenth wealthiest town in England[102]. Strange as it may seem today, its total valuation exceeded that of county towns like Gloucester, Lincoln and even York. Lavenham paid the then huge sum of £179 13s 0d, which easily outstripped its nearest local rivals, Sudbury paying £61 and Melford £65. Out of Lavenham's total the widow and daughter of Thomas Spring III contributed £66 13s 4d, or 37%. At his death in 1523, Thomas III owned property in the four counties of Suffolk, Norfolk, Essex and Cambridgeshire; his scattered estate consisted of twenty-six manors and numerous houses and pieces of land in about seventy-six other parishes. The greatest concentration of his property was, understandably, in the western half of Suffolk[103]. In 1522 he owned property in Lavenham to the value of only £20, but his movable possessions (stock-in-trade, furnishings, valuables, etc.) were worth the enormous sum of £1,800.

However, the value of the Spring estate

Left: *Molet House in Barn Street is an excellent example of a clothier's house, built in the early sixteenth century with close studding, jetties and oriel windows. Notice the large door, wide enough to take a loaded pack-animal yet with an inner personal opening.*

Opposite page: *Thomas Spring II, who died in 1486, left the first specific bequest (300 marks or £200) to the rebuilding of the church tower, so his merchant's mark and initials were carved several times around its base.*

should not obscure the fact that many other prosperous families existed in the town. Eight other Lavenham men, all clothiers, paid £5 or more to the subsidy, whereas in the rest of the large and populous Babergh Hundred only twelve other people paid a comparable amount. This underlines Lavenham's importance as a place where employers tended to congregate. Without the Spring contribution, Lavenham would have remained easily the richest place in Babergh, but it would have sunk considerably in the national ranking. As Hoskins has pointed out, the existence of one enormously rich merchant like William Wyggeston of Leicester, Richard Marler of Coventry or Thomas Horton of Bradford-on-Avon was a common pattern in English towns. Although Thomas Spring III was the richest man in provincial England outside the nobility, the contributions of other top-ranking towns were similarly boosted[104].

The amounts of tax paid in 1524 enable us to show the overall distribution of wealth in Lavenham. Of course, enormous disparities are visible, but several groups can be isolated: first the inheritors of the Spring estate; secondly a small group of very prosperous clothiers and businessmen of whom William Rysby, Robert Grome and Thomas Sexten were outstanding; thirdly a group of about twenty-five businessmen who paid more than £1 in tax; and fourthly a large group of artisans, labourers and servants who made up the vast bulk of the population. A hundred and one people paid tax on wages of £1 to £2 a year, while thirty-three others paid on wages of £2 to £3 a year; they were never wealthy enough to leave wills but they provided the essential labour, both skilled and unskilled, which supported the cloth industry and other crafts and trades, as well as local agriculture. We must also remember that other local families with an income of less than £1 a year undoubtedly existed, exempt from tax, but they need not have been a large group; a recent writer has suggested that "little more than one in ten" of the rural population of Babergh lived in conditions of extreme poverty[105].

Disturbances and Abuses 4

LAVENHAM reached a peak of prosperity in the decade which saw the death of Thomas Spring III, the completion of the church and the building of the fine Corpus Christi gildhall and many domestic properties. It was a peak of prosperity which was confirmed by the tax returns of 1524.

It is not until the second half of the sixteenth century that we are aware of any dramatic decline in Lavenham's fortunes. The registers continue to yield the wills of successful clothiers, most of them proved in the Prerogative Court of Canterbury (PCC). Between 1530 and 1560, twenty-five clothiers' wills were proved, twenty of them in the PCC, beside those of a dyer, a fuller and a mercer. We know also that Henry Tooley and other Ipswich merchants were still supplying Lavenham clothiers with imported raw materials and wines[106]. But the discontent which erupted from time to time might well have contributed to the eventual decline.

The scale of taxation in the years 1523–27, and its severity on the wealthier classes, including at least fifteen Lavenham clothiers who had to pay an additional "Anticipation", drew an angry reaction which might have proved disastrous. No doubt both clothiers and workers exaggerated their grievances, but there seems to have been a real danger of commercial retrenchment and widespread unemployment. In the spring of 1525 those put off work by the clothiers, and others threatened with unemployment, rose in protest on a large scale. The chronicler Edward Hall wrote that demonstrators at Sudbury and Lavenham numbered four thousand and that alarm bells were sounded[107].

The gravity of the crisis is underlined by a sequence of letters (perhaps "despatches" would be the more appropriate word) between Cardinal Wolsey and the Dukes of Norfolk and Suffolk, through whose efforts the threat was eventually defused. Lavenham was identified as the main centre of unrest: "the confederacy of the evil-disposed persons of this town has extended to many places in this county, Essex and Cambridgeshire, and the town and university of Cambridge"[108]. It was John Spring, eldest son of Thomas Spring III, who, together with Sir Thomas Jermyn of nearby Rushbrooke, was chosen by the dukes to warn the rioters of the dire consequences of high treason. Things quietened down, and some inhabitants of Lavenham and neighbouring Brent Eleigh came to the dukes "in their shirts and kneeled for mercy", saying that they had misbehaved "for lack of work"[109]. In 1527 seven of "the most substantial men of Lavenham" reported on oath that none in Lavenham had since misbehaved himself "except one John Porter, whom they had put out of town"[110].

Nevertheless by 1528 the clamour of protesting tradesmen again threatened the peace of the area. The trouble stemmed from the reported detention of English cloth merchants in Flanders. The consequent refusal of London merchants to buy Suffolk cloth meant that in May the clothiers felt unable to keep their

Never a priory as such, the fine complex of medieval buildings today known as The Priory belonged for centuries to the Benedictine monks of Earls Colne in Essex. It consists of an open-hall house with various additions behind and towards the street. Notice the surviving decorative plasterwork or pargeting on the exterior. This was a working farm until quite recently, but the house itself fell into serious neglect. Since 1979 a painstaking and impressive restoration has been carried out by Alan and Gwenneth Casey, and the house is now open to the public.

people at work for more than two or three weeks. The scarcity of Spanish oil was quoted as another difficulty. Cardinal Wolsey therefore put pressure on the London merchants to take the cloth, quoting the king's displeasure and discounting the rumours[111].

At this time a surprising connection is revealed between the cloth industry and new religious ideas. In the years 1508–29 the Rector of Lavenham was one Dr Stockhouse. In 1528 he was shown by a London draper called Humphrey Monmouth certain books which had been sent from the Continent by none other than the zealous reformer William Tyndale; they included his translation of the New Testament which had been denounced by the

English bishops on publication in 1526. Stock-house reportedly found no fault in these books, which presumably means that he approved of their Lutheran and Protestant ideas. For this kind of illegal importing and for his contacts with Tyndale, Monmouth, a well-known Protestant sympathizer, was thrown into prison. In a petition to Wolsey he revealed that he traded extensively in Suffolk cloth, and that while he was languishing in prison his business was collapsing. He "buys cloth, paying for them weekly, and if the clothiers fail of their money, they cannot set the poor folks to work . . . [He] usually sells 400 or 500 cloths every year to foreigners . . . most between Christmas and Whitsuntide, but he has only sold 22 since

Christmas this year, and no one asks for them"[112].

In 1536 the clothing towns were again on the brink of rebellion. An Act fixing the breadth of ordinary cloth was so bitterly resented by clothiers and their workmen that it was feared they might join the northern rebellion, which began in Lincolnshire and the north and became the occasion for airing a whole parcel of grievances ranging from taxation to enclosures. The Duke of Norfolk, again with the help of John Spring, Sir Thomas Jermyn and others, took firm measures, setting "such order that it shall be hard for anyone to speak an unfitting word without being incontinently [immediately] taken and sent to me". He recruited 1,500 "tall men out of Suffolk" who could be ready at an hour's warning, and added that if the Earl of Oxford made sure of his town of Lavenham, the rest of south-west Suffolk would be safe. This is an interesting reminder of the continuing power and prestige of the local lord, and the leading position which Lavenham and its clothiers held in the district during the first half of the sixteenth century[113].

An important Clothing Act was passed in 1551–52. It was largely a comprehensive restatement of previous legislation and codes, and, covering every branch of the trade and every type of cloth, was clearly intended to be the final and binding word on the conduct and standards of the industry. It incidentally revealed a whole range of abuses and fraudulent practices. Coloured long cloths from Norfolk, Suffolk and Essex had to be, when wet, between 28 and 30 yards long, at least 1.75 yards (5 feet 3 inches) broad, and to weigh at least 80 lb apiece. Short cloths were to be between 23 and 25 yards long, "as last remembered" in breadth, and to weigh at least 64 lb each. There was to be no straining or stretching beyond one yard in length and one-eighth of a yard in width, and no "engines" were to be used for this. Hot pressing was forbidden, as was the addition of "flox, solace, chalk, flower [sic] or any other deceitful thing" (presumably to give the cloth a false body). Sealers or inspectors were to be appointed at a fee of 2d a

cloth, and the authorities of each town were to be fined if the sealers failed to seal with an "F" and declare the fault of any cloth which was "cockley, pursey, bandy, squally, rewy, evil-burled, wasted in the Mill or full of holes". No cloth was to be made of any colour except "skarlett, redd, crymsen, murrey, violet, puke, browne, blewe, blackes, grenes, yallowes, blewes, orrige, tawnye, russett, marble, grey, sadnewcolor, asewer, watchett, shepes color, lyon color, motteley, or Iren grey". Wools to be made into broadcloths or kerseys were not to be boiled with "any kind of galles, rynds, barks of trees or sawdust"[114]. Coupled with this Act was another which limited the times of buying and selling wool, and tried to prevent

48

its hoarding against shortages and higher prices[115].

However much light this legislation sheds on the tricks of the trade, it by no means stopped the abuses, as later documents reveal. The immediate and predictable reaction of local clothiers was to complain that the cloth made by their growing rivals, the Dutch, was subject to no such restrictions and was therefore more competitive. The Dutch products were becoming more fashionable and were soon to replace broadcloth as the principal local manufacture. Modifications to the Clothing Act were introduced as soon as 1556–57, and within a few

years infringements and abuses were again widespread. Later, Suffolk broadcloth exported to Russia, the Baltic and North Africa was exempted from rules governing the limits of stretching[116]. Perhaps it was thought that these buyers would be less discerning.

Meanwhile over three consecutive years, 1553–55, certain clothiers including Nicholas Spring, John Woder and John Whyteloke of Lavenham, were granted licences to make 1,100 "sett cloths" made of coarse and refuse wool for sale to Richard Cragge, draper of London. He in turn was licensed to ship them within one year, notwithstanding the earlier statute which forbade this trade, from any port to Denmark and the Baltic, paying customs to the Crown. The condition imposed was that Cragge should bring back "cables, cordage, oars and such other furniture and munitions for ships" and sell them to the Royal Navy at reasonable prices[117]. The details of this deal which "bent the rules" have a familiar ring. In previous years coarse wool was said to have been deceitfully "indraped" into finer cloth.

Thanks to the Reformation, the magnificent Gildhall of Corpus Christi in the Market Place, the headquarters of a local religious gild, was made redundant less than thirty years after it was built in about 1520. The use of timber is almost prodigal, far more than is structurally necessary. An extensive restoration was carried out in the nineteen-twenties by the Quilter family.

Leake's *Treatise on the Cloth Industry with Proposals for the Reform of Abuses*, which appeared in 1577, disclosed widespread infringement of the Acts and expressed the fear that lowered standards would bring international disrepute and lead to the decline of cloth exporting. Leake was one of the searchers at the cloth market of Blackwell Hall mentioned above (p. 26). No branch of the trade nor any cloth-making district escaped his censure. One of two Suffolk offenders accused by name was the clothier Wyncoll from Little Waldingfield, a village close to Lavenham[118].

The searchers of Blackwell Hall kept a detailed record of the shortcomings of cloth offered for sale. This included the clothier's name, the town from which he came, the type of cloth which was found to be defective, and the amount of fine imposed. G. D. Ramsey, who examined and transcribed these documents, thought that in all probability the lists included the names of all the leading capitalist cloth manufacturers in the kingdom. The longest list covers the year from September, 1561, to September, 1562, when 372 cases were recorded. Of the offenders, eighty (about 21%) came from Kent; sixty-six (about 18%) from Gloucestershire; thirty-nine (about 10%) from Wiltshire; and twenty-seven (about 7%) from Suffolk, the fourth most common county. The places mentioned in Suffolk were as follows:

Nayland	4 clothiers
Hadleigh, Sudbury and Boxford	3 clothiers each
Ipswich, Glemsford and Edwardstone	2 clothiers each
Bury St Edmunds, Stoke-by-Nayland, Needham, Stratford & Lamfforde [?Long Melford]	1 clothier each
Unspecified places in Suffolk (NB *none* from Lavenham)	3 clothiers

Although this evidence is very negative and inconclusive, it does seem to confirm Lavenham's low profile in the third quarter of the sixteenth century[119].

We can again look specifically at Lavenham in 1568 when another lay subsidy was demanded from those who were worth £1 or more a year in lands or £3 or more in goods[120]. Because this tax was widely evaded, the returns are properly considered unreliable evidence for the assessment of local wealth. Nevertheless, unless we believe that Lavenham's evasions were hugely worse than those elsewhere in Suffolk, we need not hesitate to make rough comparisons nor to draw up a table of *relative* wealth.

The return for Lavenham lists only twenty-six names, and the total of tax paid was £7 7s 0d. This sum was less than the individual payments of Stoke-by-Nayland, Boxford, Bures (largely boosted by the contribution of Sir William Waldegrave), Long Melford, Glemsford, Sudbury and Lawshall (although the last included a large sum from the Lady Drury). It placed Lavenham only eighth in Babergh Hundred and as low as forty-ninth in the whole of Suffolk. Among the town's taxpayers, eight men can be identified as being involved in the cloth industry. The richest of these, Roger Ruggell, was taxed on goods worth £20; John Woder and John Whatlock each had £15 in goods; Nicholas Springe had £10; Edward Smythe had £8; Robert Woder and Robert Lynche each had £5; Thomas Ruggell had a mere £3 in goods. Whatever reservations are made concerning the validity of such returns, these men were not rich by the standards of Lavenham's heyday about fifty years earlier. The clothiers John Wyncoll of Little Waldingfield and Edward Coleman of Great Waldingfield each paid more than any of them[121].

A decline in the number of clothiers' wills shows the same trend, and it is clear that Lavenham's fortunes were waning considerably by the fifteen-sixties. Among the external factors which might have contributed were legislation in favour of monopolistic companies and the difficulties of keeping continental markets open. Paradoxically the decline might also have owed something to the outstanding position held earlier in the century by several

A late-nineteenth-century view of High Street. The Swan "commercial hotel" with its yawning carriage entrance has a generally dilapidated air.

very rich and successful merchant families. W. G. Hoskins has drawn attention to the fact that wealthy business families seldom remained ascendant for more than three generations[122]. Presumably by that time the business might have failed or the family run out of heirs, or, most likely, its members had acquired enough property to live on the proceeds and move into the ranks of the landed gentry, usually away from the scene of their industrial origins. The latter is observable in Lavenham's case, and the process may well have left the town poorer in reserves of capital, business connections and commercial experience.

John, the eldest son of Thomas Spring III, was already a "Gentleman" in 1524; he had married into the ancient and important Waldegrave family at Bures and was to be knighted at the accession of Edward VI. The other son, Robert, although he kept an interest in the clothing business, was also a "Gentleman" when he died in 1549 and had considerable property. The Spring daughters "married well": Margaret married Sir Thomas Jermyn of Rushbrooke, Bridget married Sir Henry Husse and their cousin Margaret married Aubrey de Vere, second son of the 15th Earl of Oxford. The family seat was afterwards established at Pakenham, fifteen miles from Lavenham in the north of the county, whence came a succession of county sheriffs. One of these, Sir William Spring, had the signal honour of meeting and escorting Queen Elizabeth I on her progress through Suffolk in 1578. The contemporary account of this progress makes no mention of Lavenham, but at Long Melford great festivities took place when the Queen visited the Hall[123]. In 1641 Sir William Spring III was created a baronet by Charles I, and the title survived until 1769[124].

Other known examples of successful Lavenham clothiers who had made the social grade include Robert Crytofte, gentleman, who died in 1560, John Grome, gentleman, who died in 1587, and Thomas Rysby, gentleman, who died in 1568 and whose family settled in Thorpe Morieux as lords of the manor. Other clothier families like the Sextens, the Sturmynes and the Braunches, whose names faded from Lavenham's records, had left the town, perhaps for landed estates elsewhere. Even the de Veres were to end their 500-year patronage of the town when in Elizabethan times the spendthrift 17th Earl of Oxford sold their manor of Lavenham to Alderman Skinner of London.

Vain and flimsy fabrics

The biggest blow to the broadcloth trade, from which Lavenham never completely recovered, was the advent of the so-called New Draperies. These new products and techniques were brought to England in the early years of Queen Elizabeth's reign by Dutch immigrants fleeing from Spanish oppression. Hard-working Protestant communities were soon established in certain eastern towns including Braintree, Colchester and Norwich, and their methods rapidly affected the traditional English industry. A contemporary, William Harrison, who was rector of Radwinter in north-west Essex, wrote as follows:

> In time past the use of this commodity [wool] consisted (for the most part) in cloth and worsteds; but now by means of strangers succoured here from domestical persecution, the same hath been employed unto sundry other uses, as mockadoes, bays, velures, grograines, etc. whereby the makers have reaped no small commodity[125].

The refugees brought with them techniques

The Dutch Quarter of Colchester, where Protestant immigrants from the Low Countries settled in the reign of Elizabeth I, having fled from Spanish persecution. Many were connected with the New Draperies.

for producing an enormous range of materials new to the English industry, described by broadcloth makers as "flimsy", but which became fashionable and in great demand. The basis of the new materials was a longer, coarser type of wool which had to be combed, unlike the short wool used to weave broadcloth, which was carded. This yarn from combed wool was mixed in the weave with a variety of other threads and fibres, and subjected to new processes such as sizing to add lustre and resilience. A bewildering range of materials was produced (see Appendix 5). Salzman and Kerridge each name about fifty of these fabrics and even their lists are not comprehensive[126]. After a specialized study of East Anglian draperies, J. E. Pilgrim had to confess that "to describe these fabrics accurately is no easy matter, and even contemporaries were at times bewildered by them"[127]. Certainly definitions vary considerably[128]. Perhaps we can best distinguish the types of material that new fashions demanded, or the fashions that the new materials introduced, by studying contemporary portraits[129].

D. C. Coleman has convincingly demonstrated that the New Draperies had their true origin in Italy[130]. The techniques developed there were later copied and exploited in Flanders, where textile manufacturers were keen to capture new markets, especially in warmer southern Europe, in the face of strong competition from English exporters. The new materials used far less wool in each cloth and were therefore generally lighter and cheaper; this meant that they could attract a wider market, including less affluent people, and could induce a greater demand for replacement than the more durable and weather-resistant broadcloth. It was against this background that English authorities had constantly sought to impose and maintain high standards on the broadcloth industry, causing clothiers to complain of their foreign rivals' unfair advantage in being free of such regulations. Now, through the "accidents" of war and religious persecution, the competition with the broadcloth industry was also growing

SUFFOLK MAKERS OF BROADCLOTH, 1558–1640	
[from J. E. Pilgrim, 'The cloth industry in Essex and Suffolk, 1558–1640', M.A. (London) thesis, 1940, 227–232]	
Town	No. of names appearing in the records from 1558 to 1640
Hadleigh	81
Boxford	67
East Bergholt	47
Nayland	41
Ipswich	24
Edwardstone	21
Lavenham	21
Stoke-by-Nayland	17
Bury St Edmunds	14
Bildeston	13
Sudbury	13
Long Melford	6
Bures	6

rapidly from within our own shores, and still free of restrictions.

The new manufacture boomed in Colchester and later spread to other centres in North Essex and along the River Stour, including Sudbury, where according to Defoe, writing much later, "a great manufacture of sayes and perpetuanas" eventually developed[131]. By 1577 the clothiers of Suffolk (that is, the makers of broadcloth as opposed to the new "stuffs") were forced to accept that the New Draperies, which they called "slight and vain", were nevertheless products "wherein the common people delight"[132].

After the arrival of the "strangers" the older industry continued and was indeed to survive for a long time, but it now supplied more restricted markets and probably played a role complementary to, rather than in competition with, the New Draperies. The chief outlets were through the Eastland and Muscovy

Companies to markets in northern Europe and even Asia, and to places which experienced continental winters.

Chiefly from recorded infringements of the code of standards, a common enough aberration at some time in a clothier's career, Pilgrim has compiled a list of broadcloth-makers working in Suffolk betwen 1558 and 1640. Lavenham's total of twenty-one names is less than that of Hadleigh, Boxford, East Bergholt, Nayland or Ipswich. The comparatively small numbers of names against Sudbury and Long Melford reflect not the honesty of their clothiers but their adoption of the manufacture of New Draperies. Hadleigh, with an impressive eighty-one names, was exceptional in still having a thriving broadcloth industry, a fact confirmed by the large number of Hadleigh wills in the PCC during this period[133].

Suffolk manufacturers of broadcloth complained that baymakers hoarded and re-sold wool, thus forcing up the price, but by the end of the sixteenth century some of their own kind were employing the same tricks. In 1593 a Lavenham clothier called George Rugle, who was described as "a great occupier in making of cloth there", was accused of re-selling 160 stone of wool to a Stowmarket man. It did him

little good, for by 1599 a George Ruggles of Lavenham (presumably the same) was declared bankrupt[134].

An improvement seems to have occurred at the end of the sixteenth century, allowing some Lavenham clothiers to do a fair volume of business. Again we have to rely on examples brought to our notice through clothiers' short-comings rather than their achievements. For example, Roger Ruggles, mentioned earlier in connection with his misuse of logwood dye, was clearly trading on a large scale, for he had dyed wool to the value of £1,000 when charged in 1592; and John Barker's debt of £90 for indigo also indicates a fairly extensive business[135].

About this time a case against London aulnagers was brought by forty clothiers, mostly from Suffolk. The aulnagers were accused of ambushing pack trains and seizing packs of cloth to extort unjust payment. Among the clothiers concerned were Roger Kerrington, John Kerrington, George Ruggles and Robert Wooder, all of Lavenham[136]. The struggle against London-based authority seems to have continued.

It is interesting that among Lavenham wills, although we have those of *earlier* members of the Ruggles, Woder and Barker families, we

In a principal room at the Old Grammar School, Barn Street, this superb frieze of shields and angels dates from c1500. The initial 'W' must refer to the original, unknown owner. Mouldings are common in the houses of Lavenham, but figurative carvings are quite rare.

have none for the six clothiers mentioned above. If they left wills, it must mean that they later moved away, either to retire or to set up business elsewhere. It is even possible that while their businesses were in Lavenham, their homes were not. This may be true of the Kerringtons, who are known to have lived in neighbouring parishes.

In 1608 Roger Grome of Lavenham was appointed one of the twenty associates of a new Clothmakers' Company, set up to maintain standards in Bury St Edmunds and the surrounding area, while JPs were empowered to punish offenders[137]. For the clothiers of Babergh and their workers, however, anxious times lay ahead.

The Tithe Map of 1843 depicts Lavenham in some detail. The town's shape had probably changed little since the Middle Ages, though many houses had sprouted extensions and outbuildings. Inexpicably, the church is not drawn. The Market Place was more built over than we see today. [SRO(B): T81/2]

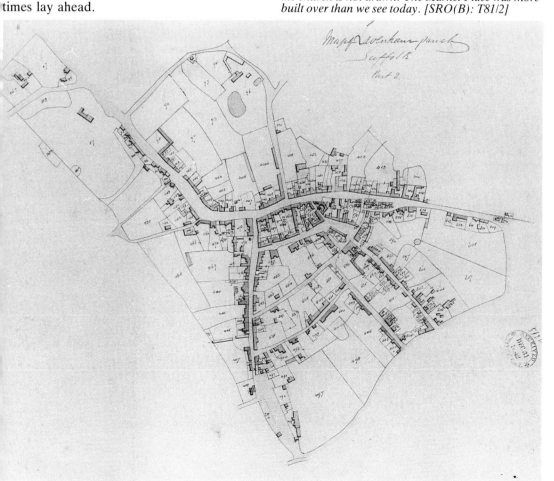

A true & perfit Inventory of all & singuler the goods &
chattells of Thomas Goodridge, late of Lavinham in the
county of Suff deceased, taken & apprized the 10th of
July 1660: by John Gale & Thomas Steward; Apprizers

Imprimis in ready money & wearing Apparrell   453-0-0

In the parlour, one poste bedstedle, with
greene Curtaines & vallance, 2 fether bedds, 1 flock
bed & strawbed, 3 fether bolsters, 1 flock bolster,
2 pillowes, & 1 old coverlid   7-0-0

Item one livery Cubberd, 2 old boxes, & 1 joyned
chayer, & 3 small chayers, & 1 old wicker chayer   0-16-0

Item one silver guilt spoone, & 3 silver spoones —   0-16-0

Item 21 pewter dishes, 4 sawsers, 1 porringer, 2 pewter
boults, 1 pewter tankerd, 1 lattin Cullender, 1 sawcepan,
& 1 tunnill   3-0-0

Item 3 brasse Candlestick, & 1 plate Candlestick,
& 1 lattin Candlestick   0-4-0

Item one paire of Andirons wth firepan &
tonguds with brasse heades   0-6-8

Item 4 paines & 1 old Course sheet, & 1 paire of fine
sheets, & 3 paire of fine yillow sheets —   2-0-0

Item 2 board clothes, 8 napkins, & 2 towells   0-10-0

Item 2 doss: of trenchers   0-1-0

Item 1 book of martirs, 1 bible, & other bookes   1-0-0

In the Hall & the roome by it:
Item 1 table, 1 chest, & 1 box   0-12-0
Item 1 forke, & 1 spitt   0-10-0
Item 5 painted bookes   0-5-0
Item 3 brasse pottes & 2 skillites   0-10-0

In an old Chamber
2 old chestes, & 1 old bedstedle   0-5-0

In the wooll Chamber
In fine yarne 44 grosse at 16s 7d   35-4-0
Item in sey yarne 20 gross & 10 doss: at 16d   16-13-4
Item in midle wooll 84lb at 4d   02-16-0
Item in sey wooll 14 stoane at 9s 6d   10-10-0
Item in cloathing wooll, 9 stoane & 5lb at 7s 6d   06-2-6
Item in mylled 11 stoane at   03-0-0
Item 4 runn: of oyle & a little fine wooll   04-0-0
Item 1 Iron beame wt. deep scoales & weights wt.
lead: 3 96lb one 28lb two 14 2 7 1 Iron 14lb   02-0-0
Item in Course corke   01-10-0
Item 3 sugarloves at 26d a peece   03-10-0
Item 2 haurbe loakes   00-6-0
Item in Course yarne 5d   00-8-0
Item in hey, in the barne & wood   02-10-0
Item one mare & sadle   02-5-0
Item in mow likeing   02-10-0
Item one peece of wt. Tamie left for   02-0-0
Item 1 peece of sad Coullerdyed stoane   02-2-0
Item 2 stoabon round weights now   00-2-4
Item 16 toppes at the spinsters in towne   01-1-4
Item att the spinsters in Cambridge shiere
11 gross 4 doss: & halfe of yarne at 16s 7d   09-2-0
Item in 20lb Clothyd Coppd in Cambridgshire 00   10-0-0
Item hear Coppd of 20s a peece given by will to his wife 60   0-0
Item in other debts hopefull   569-15-2
Item debts doubtfull & desparat   052-1-1

                              Sum total 1261-3-4

John Gale
Tho: Steward

192

Decay and Change 5

CORRESPONDENCE between the local justices and the Privy Council in the sixteen-twenties repeatedly refers to "the decay of clothing" and the "great distress thereby fallen upon the weavers, spinners and fullers . . . for want of work". Indeed, we have considerable documentary evidence for depression and poverty in the clothing centres of the Babergh area in this period, although we cannot spotlight Lavenham specifically.

Clothiers complained that prices were ruinously low and that they had many unsold cloths on their hands. They blamed the situation on monopolistic corporations, the bankruptcy of some merchants and the effect of high duties. In 1622 a total of 4,453 cloths worth £39,282 remained unsold in twenty Suffolk townships, while the clothiers of twelve townships had lost £30,415 in five years because of bankruptcies. Many clothiers had gone out of business[138]. In this time of scarcity and want of work, the poorer spinners of Babergh were also in a sorry plight, being deprived of work by the wives of better-off farmers[139].

No doubt recalling the rebellions of impoverished clothing workers in the past, and fearing trouble, the Council promised measures at a national level; by raising public stocks they hoped to take unsold cloths off clothiers' hands, to restrain growers from forcing up the price of wool and to provide work for unemployed weavers, spinners and fullers. Little, however, seems to have been achieved.

In 1638 a Royal Commission was appointed to inquire into the state of the clothing industry and to recommend measures for its reformation. Its report was a familiar recital and indictment of malpractices in all branches of the industry. However, it may never have been considered by the Privy Council, for it was published at the time when relations between King and Parliament had brought the country to the brink of civil war. The commissioners recommended the granting of incorporations to all the chief clothing towns, whose officers would be responsible for "the well-ordering and government of the manufacture". Annexed was a list of clothing towns deemed "considerable for this work". In nineteen counties sixty-two towns were listed; those mentioned in Suffolk were Ipswich, Hadleigh, St Edmundsbury, Sudbury, Barford (East Bergholt), Groton and Nayland. Even in this lean period it is difficult to think that Lavenham was considered less significant than all of these, but it was not mentioned[140].

Notwithstanding the low state of Lavenham's industry in the first half of the seventeenth century, it would be wrong to see this as the end of the town's reliance on clothmaking. Although at this time Lavenham produced a higher proportion of wills from rich yeomen farmers, for whose products the ever-growing population of London no doubt provided the best markets, it also yielded a sparse but persistent succession of wills from clothiers. After 1648 continental markets, which had been disrupted and made hazardous by the Thirty Years' War, became once more accessible and this may have helped towards a modest recovery.

It is uncertain to what extent Lavenham's clothmakers took up the manufacture of New Draperies in the first half of the seventeenth century, but no evidence exists for any significant change. In 1622 a petition was presented by "the makers of bays and says, stuffs and fustians, commonly called the New Draperies, within the counties of Essex, Suffolk and Norfolk, to the Privy Council for redress against intruders in the said trade"[141]. Clearly a change would have had to be made in the teeth of collective opposition. Thomas Taylor of Lavenham may have been one such intruder, for his will, proved in 1626, described him as a baymaker. This is the first reference to the New Draperies in Lavenham. Taylor appears to have been of somewhat meagre means, however, and no other such specialists are recorded before the Restoration of King Charles II in 1660, unless we include Ambrose Pricke, who was a feltmaker and died in 1631[142].

After 1660 there followed a comparatively, but only comparatively, prosperous period based largely on New Draperies. Perhaps the half-century or so following the Restoration can best be summarized by quoting Richard Blomes's *Britannia* of 1673: "In the southern track [of Suffolk] the great, but *decaying*, trade is in broadcloth for beyond sea, the western [that is, West of England] cloths having outstript [them]." But of Lavenham he writes that it is "a large clothing town enjoying a pretty good trade, having a good market on Tuesdays, which is the more frequented by reason of a famous Lecture [weekly sermon] there". (William Jacob's cross in the Market Place was the pulpit for this regular Tuesday sermon, and for other public announcements until well into the nineteenth century.) Although the Suffolk cloth trade was in decline, Lavenham was moderately prosperous and its population probably peaked at this time[143].

For a closer look at this temporary revival, reference can be made to a series of probate inventories which are among our best sources for the social and economic history of Lavenham. They are lists of the movable goods and assets of those recently deceased, and were drawn up by local people for the ecclesiastical courts as part of the business of proving wills. Altogether 118 of these documents survive for Lavenham. This may seem a large number, but their use is limited by various factors. First, although they range in date from 1486 to 1795, they are not spread out evenly during those three hundred years. The vast majority (102 out of 118) fall within the sixty years from 1660 to 1720; indeed, a third of the total number come from a single decade, 1660–70. Secondly, the number of inventories clearly represents only a tiny fraction of the total population. Even for the period 1660 to 1720, the 102 surviving inventories represent under 3% of all the people who died and are mentioned in the burial register (including children). Furthermore there is undoubtedly a social bias.

The total values of the Lavenham inventories prove the last point: eighty-six list goods above the value of £20, mostly well above this value; only fourteen inventories total under £10 and therefore represent the worldly goods of relatively poor people. Edward Beare can be taken as an example of the last category. He lived in Potterland near the church, and his goods in 1680 were valued at only £3 8s 6d. Two beds, two tables and two hutches (chests) with a few hearth implements and cooking utensils were virtually all he had[144]. Most people like him probably never made a will, and so no inventories were written after their deaths. The poor in Lavenham, as shown by the returns to the Hearth Tax of 1674, made up over half of the population[145].

One thing which a study of inventories does emphasize is the strongly commercial and industrial character of old Lavenham. Whereas purely agricultural communities produce relatively large numbers of inventories for those whose sole occupation was on the land, mostly called husbandmen and yeomen, Lavenham has produced only twelve inventories of farmers. The rest, many of whom admittedly did some farming, were primarily engaged in a

Two working tower mills on Mill Hill in the late nineteenth century, a view which reminds us of the farming involvements which have always been part of Lavenham's economy. Only the base of one of the mills survives.

wide range of industries, crafts and trades.

Clothiers and wool-dealers constituted by far the wealthiest group. Ten of their inventories survive, all within the period 1664–1709, with an average total value of £605, but this figure conceals a very wide range of wealth. At one end of the scale William Canham, who died in 1680, left goods totalling only £60 5s 6d in value. At the other end were three individuals who each had moveables worth over £1,000. Thomas Goodridge (died 1668) was worth £1,261 3s 4d, Nicholas Wells (died 1667) was worth £1,659 14s 7d, and William Wiles senior (died 1666) had moveables to the value of £2,180 7s 0d[146].

Interestingly only one of these ten men appeared to have looms at his home, which suggests that they mainly dealt in wool, yarn and cloth and organized craftsmen working in

their own homes. For example, Thomas Goodridge is mentioned as having spinners working on his wool in Lavenham and in Cambridgeshire, while John Kegus had wool in "spin-houses" at Stanton (?Cambs. or Suffolk) and at "Eselum" (?Isleham, Cambs.). The business of these men was undoubtedly still dependent on large amounts of credit because over half of their wealth, as expressed in the inventories, was in the form of debts due to them.

The three wealthiest producers, mentioned above, all died within a period of three years. They probably mark the highest point of the New Draperies in Lavenham in the mid-to-late seventeenth century and could be regarded as the counterparts of those wealthy clothiers of the late fifteenth and sixteenth centuries, such as William Rysby, William Jacob and Thomas Spring III, who had been concerned with the old broadcloth industry in its heyday. It is worth noting that both these enterprising groups were called "clothiers", so the word cannot be taken as definitely implying either the Old or New Draperies.

Also in the second half of the seventeenth century, we have the inventories of four

workers in the cloth industry, representing the craftsmen who did the manual labour. One is specified as a saymaker, one a worsted weaver, another simply as a weaver, and the last is clearly a shearman. Although their average wealth is £145, well below that of the clothier-dealers, three of them were as well off as the lesser members of the first group. Indeed the worsted weaver, John Tarver, who died in 1696, had movable goods of greater value than six of the organizers. The really significant thing about the workers is that they were more directly involved in the industrial processes. Not only were Tarver's warehouse and chambers full of wool, yarn and cloth, but attached to his house were workshops with at least nine looms in them (see Appendix 5). This is the nearest we get in Lavenham's early history to a factory.

Seventeenth-century inventories give far more detail about local industries than do wills, and the cloth industry is revealed in nearly all its processes. Wool itself was described either by appearance (small, short), by its form (fleeces, cast, skin, tops) or by its suitability for particular kinds of cloth (say, hanwarp, clothing, grey woolsey). Sometimes very large quantities were stored in "woolchambers", which were presumably upper rooms with external doors and hoists. For example, Nicholas Wells had wool "in the fleece and ready cast" to the value of £500 in his woolchambers. Yarn, too, was described according to its fineness or suitability for specified kinds of cloth; some was said to be greasy and some scoured. As might be expected, yarn was either "at home" or "abroad" with the spinners. The equipment used by wool dealers and combers included "rings" or wringers for scouring wool, combs, combing pots and charcoal for heating combs, "white soap", lead cisterns, oil kettles, tubs and baskets. John Wells who died in 1685 had a special scouring shop which contained "scouring winches", tubs and pails. Among the devices used by yarnmakers and weavers were stock-cards, twisting mills with bobbins, warping mills and warping bars with pins for preparing yarn for the loom. Looms at this date still included "broad" and "narrow", and generally cost less than £1.

Among the categories of cloth produced in Lavenham were says, serges, calamancoes, tammies, "cottons" and antherines. The only kind of dye mentioned was "grain colour", but it may not have been the genuine red dye derived from a Mediterranean insect. Most of the equipment connected with cloth finishing came from Francis Cannum's inventory of 1669; he possessed six shears, a quantity of handles and frames, "cottening boards" for raising the nap of cloth, shear-boards, trestles and stage, brushes, tenters and a press[147]. A very common reference was to iron beams, scales and weights of lead or iron, by which wool, yarn and cloth were weighed as each craftsman collected and returned his responsibility. At this time the government appointed inspectors to travel round the country and check the accuracy of wool weights; they carried standard weights suspended from either side of their saddles. Finally we are reminded of the problems of transporting bulky goods by the mention of yarn bags, pocket cloths, "surplis cloths", pack cloths and

Right: *Clear traces of industrial processes are rarely found in Lavenham's houses, but in a house in Prentice Street carefully spaced holes, bored in rows on the studs of an internal wall, were probably used for preparing yarn as warp for a loom. The pegs themselves are modern.*

Below: *First-floor doors such as this one in Water Street were once common features in Lavenham, because upper rooms were often used to store wool, yarn and cloth.*

pack saddles. (For a glossary of contemporary terms, see pp. 125–127.)

Another distinct group comprised various craftsmen who were *not* concerned with the making of cloth. Inventories exist for two blacksmiths, two glaziers, a wheelwright, a woodworker (who specialized in sieves, taps, wooden spoons, platters, lanterns and rake-heads), a tanner, three glovers, a collar-maker and a cordwainer (usually interpreted as a shoemaker, though this man concentrated on saddlery and ropework). One of the glovers had an extensive stock, which included gloves for "workdays" and "holidays", as well as "half

Opposite page: *A woolcomber at work, from* The Book of Trades, *published in Philadelphia in 1807. The comber is dragging wool through the strong iron teeth of a comb fixed to the wall. The large pot was for heating the combs, which made it easier to draw wool through the teeth.*

Below: *Prentice Street, seen here during the celebrations of Queen Victoria's Diamond Jubilee, was in the fifteenth century the home of one of Lavenham's tanners.*

handed" gloves or mittens[148]. These leather-workers had considerable quantities of hides and skins: Richard Palmer, a glover who died in 1667, had skins of calves, sheep, lambs, does and moles[149]. In the later seventeenth century, two leather sealers were annually elected at the vestry meeting of Lavenham, so tanning and leatherworking must have been of some consequence at this time[150]. Not that it was an entirely new speciality. As early as 1441, John Swayn, who lived in Prentice Street, had been a barker or tanner: he bequeathed barkwoods, bark, barkvats and leather. John Parle, who died in 1444, was also a barker who lived in Bolton Street "next to the gate of John Swayn".

The five traders or shopkeepers whose inventories survive are, as a group, almost as wealthy as the clothier-dealers. Their inventories average £578 in value. Once again the giving of credit was normal, for on average £219 was in money due. Thomas Mayhew was the wealthiest with movable goods valued at £1,633 11s 4d. He was called a grocer, but his shop at Lavenham contained large quantities

of woollen cloth and linen; he had another shop at Cockfield and clear business connections in London. John Whiting was another grocer-cum-draper. Although his goods were worth an unspectacular £364, the inventory goes into enormous detail about the stock in his warehouse and shop. For example, six different kinds of sugar are itemized as well as exotic wares such as Smyrna raisins, cinnamon, aniseed and Sivell (Seville) oil.

The most impressive inventory of all is surely John Pinchbeck's (see Appendix 5). He was a woollen draper whose moveables were worth £420. At his death in 1704 his shop contained a hundred different kinds of cloth—all in small quantities—as well as laces, ribbons, thread, hose, handkerchiefs and other accessories. This list of local and imported cloth is a vivid reminder of the vast technical expertise which had existed in Lavenham since at least the fourteenth century. John Pinchbeck is recorded as valuer on no fewer than twelve local inventories; no doubt his special knowledge of the cloth trade was very useful on these occasions.

In spite of recurrent slumps and the decline of the Old Draperies, the population of Lavenham had risen steadily from the later sixteenth century and reached a peak of nearly 2,000 in the reign of Charles II. This estimate is based on baptisms recorded in the parish register. In 1627 Lavenham was described in the sort of language which is used to discuss modern urban problems: it was seen as "a great and populous towne, subiecte to moche disorder"[151]. From about 1680, when the second peak of prosperity was passing, the population appears to have declined, perhaps by as much as a quarter. This was probably the first serious decline since about 1400, and it went on until the middle of the eighteenth century, when some recovery is visible. The same trends have also been noticed in other manufacturing centres which were in decline, such as East Bergholt[152]. By 1778, when the first deliberate count was made of Lavenham's population, 1,741 people were living in 395 houses and tenements[153].

Woolcombing and the yarn trade

In about 1603 Robert Reyce, of Preston St Mary, the next parish to Lavenham, had written about the recent appearance of a new trade "commonly called Kembing" (that is, combing). The longer, coarser wool used to make the New Draperies needed to be bought, sorted, washed, combed and trimmed before being given to spinners who made it into fine yarn. All these processes gave work to "many of the poorer sort". The actual spinning was said to be far easier, cleaner and more profitable than comparable work in the broadcloth trade, and far more people were offering themselves at that time than could be employed. Finished yarn was carried weekly to London, Norwich and other places "where it is

ever readily sold to those who make thereof all sorts of fringes, stuffs and many other things which are at this day used and worn"[154]. It was calculated in 1738 that a pack of wool (240 lb) suitable for making broadcloth might employ sixty-three people for a week, but a pack of wool suitable for making "stuffs" could employ as many as 202, including seven combers and 150 spinners[155].

Reyce's somewhat glowing account introduces the preparatory processes which were of great importance to Lavenham's economy throughout the eighteenth century, and lingered into the nineteenth. Unfortunately we have no documentary evidence comparable with the old subsidy returns or muster roll which could give us a comprehensive picture of the occupations and economic standing of Lavenham and its neighbours during the eighteenth century. However, the general outline is fairly clear, thanks to three contemporary descriptions.

In about 1730, the Rev. Thomas Cox indicated that weaving was still continued in Lavenham, and specified "Serges, Shalloons, Says [and] Stuffs", but that the main emphasis was already on trading in wool, combing and spinning. In fact, quite apart from the ordinary market for provisions held on Tuesdays, a special market was held on Thursdays "for the traders in wool". A woolhall had been established in the town, "being mightily conveniently situated for the traders of the adjoining parts of the County". As a result "many hundred loads of wool are sold out to tradesmen in a year", and the spinning of fine yarn for London "has of late flourished more than ever"[156]. The woolhall mentioned by Cox is undoubtedly the one in Lady Street, originally the medieval hall of Our Lady's Gild. Before its timbers were re-exposed in modern times, its plastered exterior bore the date 1696; this may have marked the building's conversion into an indoor market where woolgrowers, dealers, combers, and yarnmakers could meet and bargain.

In 1764 Dr Richard Pococke passed through Lavenham and commented on its populous and bustling character. He mentioned "a Manufacture of Saies" which shows that a certain amount of cloth was still being woven, but again insisted that "a much greater" source of employment lay in the spinning of woollen yarn which was sent to both Norwich and London. "It is a very agreeable sight in the evening", he enthused, "to observe a great Number of Children in the streets, but much more to see them and the weomen imploied in spinning at six o'clock in the morning"[157]. This picture is confirmed by Mrs Ann Gilbert, who was a girl in Lavenham during the seventeen-eighties. She described "the street lined with spinning wheels (not spinning-jennies, but Jennies spinning); everywhere without, the whiz of the wheels, and within, the scrape, the clatter and thump of the loom at which the men were at work"[158].

Other scattered pieces of evidence help to substantiate these overall trends. The earliest will of a woolcomber from Lavenham was left by William Causton in 1633. He lived in a property which included the later-Georgianized "Great House" and the adjoining "Little Hall"[159]. He came of a local family who had been involved with clothmaking since the fifteenth century. However, this is the only example before 1660. The number of parish apprentices to Lavenham clothmakers also declined, only two weavers being mentioned after 1720; by contrast, the five apprenticeships to local woolcombers were all recorded after that date. Wills of the eighteenth century do not generally contain much information about occupations, but out of eighteen Lavenham wills proved in the Norwich Consistory Court between 1720 and the end of the century three belonged to fairly prosperous master woolcombers and only one to a weaver (proved as late as 1801).

A long run of forty-nine deeds relating to one important house tell the same story. No 81 Church Street, now known as Fir Tree House,

OCCUPATIONS KNOWN TO EXIST IN LAVENHAM, 1684–1780

[from Marriage Licence Bonds in SRO(B), Books I–XXII]

Occupation		Occupation		Occupation	
Apothecary (Aromatarium)	1	Gentleman	13	Saddler	1
Attorney-at-law	1	Glazier	2	Say-maker	2
Baker	3	Grocer	3	Shoe-maker	9
Barber	7	Hemp-weaver	1	Tailor	3
Basket-maker	1	Horse-dealer	1	Tallow-chandler	2
Blacksmith	5	Husbandman or Farmer	18	Tanner	3
Bricklayer	1	Innholder	7	Vintner	1
Butcher	2	Joiner	1	Weaver or Webster	8
Carpenter	4	Ironmonger	1	Wheelwright	2
Clerk	1	Labourer	3	Woolcomber or	19
Clock-maker	1	Linen draper	1	Woolstapler	
Clothier	3	Maltster	3	Woolcomb-maker	1
Collar-maker	1	Man-servant	1	Woollen-draper	1
Cooper	2	Miller	3	Worsted-weaver	2
Currier	1	Minister of the Gospel	1	Yarn-maker	1
Draper	1	Musician	1	Yeoman	19
Gardener	1	Pedlar	1		

Analysis of above occupations
(those in italics are shown in more than one category)

Textiles	clothier (3), hemp-weaver (1), say-maker (2), weaver or webster(8), woolcomber or woolstapler (19), woolcomb-maker (1) worsted-weaver (2), yarn-maker (1)	(total 37)
Leather working	collar-maker (1), currier (1), saddler (1), *shoe-maker* (9), tanner (3)	(total 15)
Metal working	blacksmith (5), clock-maker (1)	(total 6)
Wood working	basket-maker (1), *carpenter* (4), cooper (2), *joiner* (1), wheelwright (2)	(total 10)
Building	bricklayer (1), glazier (2), *carpenter* (4), *joiner* (1)	(total 8)
Making of clothes	tailor (3), *shoe-maker* (9)	(total 12)
Farming	husbandman or farmer (18), yeoman (19)	(total 37)
Preparation of food	baker (3), butcher (2), maltster (3), miller (3)	(total 11)
Retailing	draper (1), grocer (3), horse-dealer (1), ironmonger (1), linen draper (1), pedlar (1), tallow-chandler (2), vintner (1), woollen-draper (1)	(total 12)
Services	apothecary (1), attorney (1), barber (7), clerk (1), gardener (1), innholder (7), minister of religion (1), musician (1)	(total 20)
Others	gentleman (13), man-servant (1), labourer (3)	(total 17)

Fir Tree House in Church Street, one of the few in Lavenham to be handsomely Georgianized in the eighteenth century, was occupied by many people associated with the woollen trade. They include Samuel Watkinson, a wealthy woolcomber who led a nonconformist emigration to America in the seventeen-nineties.

changed hands frequently. Over the period covered by the deeds, 1612–1819, at least two dozen occupants were mentioned, with their occupations. Among them appear one weaver, three clothiers and eight woolcombers or yarnmakers. The weaver and three clothiers lived in the seventeenth century, as did three of the woolcombers; four other woolcombers were occupants in the eighteenth century, and another in the early nineteenth (but, as an illustration of the partiality of these sources, none of these individuals featured in the Norwich wills or apprenticeship indentures)[160].

The best sample of Lavenham's occupations came from marriage licence bonds covering the period 1684–1780. These bonds were entered into when a couple were to be married by special licence rather than by the announcement of banns; two named sureties guaranteed that the marriage would take place in a specified church or chapel. Many bonds specify the occupations of the main parties and of the sureties. The 171 men whose names and jobs were given belonged to no fewer than forty-two different occupations. Farming was the most common, but the next most important group consisted of nineteen woolcombers and staplers (wool sorters and dealers). Between 1684 and 1700 there are mentioned three clothiers, one saymaker, two worsted weavers, one other weaver and a woolcomber. After 1700, on the other hand, no clothiers appear but there are seven weavers, one hemp weaver, one saymaker, eighteen woolcombers and staplers, and a maker of woolcombs. Again, these names are additional to those already mentioned from other sources.

These comparatively small pieces of evidence do not allow us to estimate the total numbers of people in different trades, nor do they enable us to reconstruct the distribution of wealth. Yet they appear to fit the picture of what was happening generally in southern Suffolk where weaving and cloth-finishing, after a major decline around 1700, slowly dwindled, tending to survive only in very specialized manufactures like fustians, calamancoes and bunting. Meanwhile, woolcombing and spinning for the London and Norwich markets provided a livelihood for many and prosperity for a few. Samuel Watkinson, for example, one of the master wool-

While its elevation still betrays an open hall with parlour and service rooms, this medieval house in Shilling Street has many later features such as a massive inserted chimney stack, assorted windows and decorative plasterwork.

combers who lived in Fir Tree House, and who led a local nonconformist emigration to America in the seventeeen-nineties, was said to have been worth £30,000[161].

Quite apart from those engaged on wool, yarn and cloth, plenty of other occupations existed in the eighteenth-century town. In fact, apprenticeship indentures suggest a greater diversity of crafts than ever before: between 1700 and 1760 occupations such as cordwainers, glovemakers, wheelwright, dauber and basketmaker are mentioned for the first time as taking on apprentices. The list of occupations derived from marriage licence bonds is even more varied and includes an apothecary, currier, clockmaker, hempweaver, musician and tallow-chandler.

For the majority of local residents, however, employment did not mean prosperity. In 1776 Lavenham's expenditure on poor-relief was exceeded by only six other places in Suffolk, and all of them had larger populations: Ipswich, Bury St Edmunds, Sudbury, Woodbridge, Hadleigh and Long Melford. Its workhouse, which by an ironical twist of fate was the former Corpus Christi gildhall, had accommodation for eighty paupers[162]. It is worth noting that Lavenham was never rich enough in the eighteenth century to embark on the rebuilding of its houses. As Dr Pococke commented in 1764, "the town is large and very Populous, but old built". In fact, no eighteenth-century houses survive, and in general it is the medieval and Tudor structures which have lasted, with adaptation, from Lavenham's greatest period in the fifteenth and sixteenth centuries until the present day. At best the residents of Lavenham could afford only a new Georgian facade, in brick or plaster, masking an older timber-framed building. Even this was unusual, and only two examples are of high quality; interestingly, one of these is Fir Tree House, the home of Samuel Watkinson. In neighbouring Long Melford, considerably more work of this period is visible, reflecting no doubt its more buoyant manufacture of New Draperies and its lively coaching trade.

Right: *Shilling Grange in Shilling Street was modernized in the late seventeenth and eighteenth centuries. It is now divided into two properties; one half retains the modernization and the other was stripped and restored with a heavy hand after 1926.*

Below: *Numbers 6 and 7 Lady Street are a fine late-medieval house with a typical crown-post roof. The higher part at the far end was a new parlour built before 1556 by a clothier named John Whatlock.*

Burialls January 1711

21	Isaac son of James Watson
23	Sarah Wife of Robert Sall
25	John son of Daniel Banne
26	Abraham Grand
30	Mary Woodgate single woman
30	William son of Peter Bowers
31	Sarah Daughter of Daniel Bame

February 1711/12

1	Judeth Woodgate Wedow
2	Rebetta Wife of Daniel Banne
2	Elizabath Wife of William Southgat
3	Oliver Wife of Stephen Lanson
4	Samuel son of Samuel Day
6	Neremiah son of Samuel Bastes
7	Ruth Daughter of Gorge Sargent
10	Mary Grand Wedow
11	Samuel Alexander Junior
12	William Woodgate Junior
13	Ann daughter of Daniel Lamburd
14	Stephen Lanson Senior
15	John son of John Maken
17	Thomas Larper Jun:
18	Mary Wife of Thomas Lilbe
18	Elizabath Daughter of Roger Steed
18	Samuel Boutel Senior
19	Frances Daughter of Will Child
20	Samuel Day Senior
20	Ann Meane Wedow
23	Mary Wife of John Caste
24	Sarah Daughter of John Kilburn
25	Elizabeth Boutell
25	James son of James Lumb
25	William Southgate
26	Thomas Hop
26	Thomas Ball Senior
26	Susan Wife of John Leeke
28	John son of Andrew Bennet
28	Sarah Wife of Nicholas Danie
29	William son of Thomas Lilbe
29	Ann Wife of John Hawward

Burialls March 1711

1	Unnes Harvin a single woman
2	Mary Daughter of John Hayward
2	Mary daughter of James Lumle
3	Abraham Maken senior
6	John son of Edward Willum
6	Susan Meller single woman
7	Rebetta Wells single woman
7	Margaret Clarke a single woman
8	Thomas Green Junior
8	Ann: Wife of Samuel Alexander
8	Susan Wife of Gorge Talbut
9	John Larper Junior
10	Lawrance Borden
11	Edward Ditter Junior
13	Charles son of Mr John Culpeck
13	Daniel Lamburg Senior
18	William son of Thomas Green
18	Mary Daughter of John Sall
18	Martha daughter of John Maken
19	John son of John Breson
19	John son of Frances Lum Wedow
25	1712 Hennry son of Nathan Harvin
26	John Church a single man
27	Thomas Larper a single man
29	Mary daughter of Thomas Mills
31	Robert Lum Senior
31	Jones son of Robart Sall Junior

Aprill 1712

1	John son of John Meller Junior
3	Tamasen Daughter of Thomas Lilbe
5	Mary Wife of Joshua Harper
5	Elizabath Wife of Robert Eaton
10	Sarah Wife of Mr Samuel Elles
10	Roger Steed Senior
12	Sarah Souter
12	Samuel Staufe
13	Frances Whilborn Wedow
15	Sarah Wife of Richard Petley
15	Mary Wife of Thomas Loude
21	Elizabath Wife of John Eawerrer
23	Ann Daughter of Robert Earon
24	Ann Daughter of Mary Steed Wedow

Apprenticeship indentures provide another useful sidelight on social and economic life in the seventeenth and eighteenth centuries. For the period 1660 to 1770 Lavenham has 123 of these documents, recording how the parish arranged for some of its pauper children, doubtless including illegitimates and orphans, to be apprenticed to masters in various trades and crafts[163]. As parishes often preferred to export these children to other places, it is not surprising to find that 54% of the masters to whom Lavenham children were apprenticed lived elsewhere: 21% of them were scattered in other parts of west Suffolk, with the greatest concentration in Long Melford; 20% were in Essex, principally Colchester; and slightly under 10% were in London and Middlesex. The few remaining were in east Suffolk, Norfolk and, in one surprising case, in Ireland.

Of the Lavenham apprentices, seventy-four were to be employed in the cloth or woollen industry, mainly as weavers, in Suffolk, Essex and London. This was presumably because, even as youngsters, they would have had some acquaintance with the skills of the craft. Because farming was still the basis of the East Anglian economy, it is perhaps rather surprising to find that only six young men were apprenticed to husbandry (that is, as farm labourers). As usual, girls tended to be apprenticed to housewifery (that is, domestic service)[164].

Fifty-five masters were found from within Lavenham itself, of whom thirty-six were concerned with the manufacture of cloth or the preparation of wool and yarn. They were described as weavers of bays, says and worsteds, a feltmaker, woolcombers, and fellmongers. It is clear from the indentures that

this industry continued to be of some importance in the eighteenth century. Whereas 53% of the Lavenham masters were concerned with cloth or wool in the period from 1660 to 1700, in the next forty years 67% were so employed. Nevertheless, it is significant that before 1720 all of them were weaving cloth, whereas after that date we find only two weavers and all the woolcombers.

Like the probate inventories, the 123 surviving indentures are by no means evenly spread over time: forty-seven for the period 1660 to 1700, and sixty-three from 1700 to 1740. Of the latter it is remarkable that forty-one were signed in only ten years (1706–15) and seventeen in one particular year (1714). This peak reflects a time of economic slump and hardship during which the parish was faced with a sharp increase in the number of pauper families and orphans. These years saw not only a severe depression in the clothmaking industry but also a disastrous outbreak of smallpox. In sixteen months between August, 1711, and November, 1712, the parish register of Lavenham recorded no fewer than 259 burials—over six times the normal average—and an appeal was launched throughout western Suffolk for the relief of the town[165].

Arthur Young of nearby Bradfield Combust, the famous agricultural writer, who had been educated at Lavenham grammar school, indicated that the town's manufacture of calamancoes survived until the seventeen-nineties at least. By that time, too, Lavenham shared with other Suffolk towns a minor boom in the making of fabrics from vegetable fibres. The firm of List and Kilbourne, which suffered a serious fire in 1793, had a sizable "hemp and flax manufactory"[165a]. The making of hempen cloth may even have been stepped up during the Napoleonic Wars[166], but after 1800 local records yield very few references to weavers of any sort. By 1840, and probably well before that date, the great tradition of woollen weaving was certainly dead, after a continuous life of more than five centuries.

As might be expected, woolcombing and spinning lasted rather longer. One estimate in

Left: *A page from the parish register of Lavenham illustrating the smallpox outbreak of 1711–12. At its peak in February thirty-two burials were listed (in a normal month Lavenham expected fewer than six). Within three months, Thomas Risbe had lost his wife, son and daughter. The New Year then began on 25th March, Lady Day.*
[SRO:FL 508/4/3]

Above: *Decorative plasterwork on the Swan Hotel. The mitre may allude to St Blaise, the patron saint of woolcombers, whose feast on 3rd February was enthusiastically celebrated in Lavenham.*

Below: *A fragment of carving on the Old Grammar School in Barn Street showing a pair of human legs suggests that some, at least, of the external timbers of this fine house were meant to be seen. The insertion of a later doorcase and bay window has truncated the carving.*

the seventeen-eighties suggested that these two crafts employed more than 37,000 people in Suffolk, while in Lavenham itself in 1769 Arthur Young had referred to "many wool-combers" who earned from 12s to 14s a week and were more prosperous than those who wove says and calamancoes for an average of 5s 6d to 6s a week[167]. In 1825 a local firm still had fifty combers who celebrated Bishop Blaise's day on 3rd February with a procession and dinner[168]. Nevertheless the increasing competition of other regions and the effects of mechanization ensured that the trades of spinning and combing also declined, though they did linger on locally until the second half of the nineteenth century.

A commercial directory of 1839 listed three firms in Lavenham still concerned with the making of yarn. These are repeated in another directory of 1844, which describes Thomas Hitchcock of Prentice Street and Thomas Turner of High Street as both wool-staplers and "Worsted and Poplin yarn Manu-facturers", while Samuel Meeking in the High Street is confined to yarn making[169]. Although hand-spinning was said to be still "very brisk"

in Lavenham in 1835, other indications suggest that these businesses were not really thriving or large, and that poverty and unemployment were widespread. A Commission of 1843 stated that whereas formerly all the women and children in villages from ten to fifteen miles around Lavenham had spun yarn (earning as much as their husbands) for 150 combers, there remained in 1843 only sixteen combers, and the population was "almost purely agricultural"[170]. In 1849 W. and H. Rainbird said that the last two or three woolstaplers of Lavenham, who principally supplied yarn to Dublin for the weaving of a stuff called "tabinet", then employed about 600 spinners in Brent Eleigh, Monks Eleigh, Shimpling, Cockfield, Rattlesden and other neighbouring villages. This was a small fraction of previous numbers. Furthermore, the average housewife could not spin above two pounds a week, and at the rate of 13d per pound the earnings were "trifling". Moreover those writers reckoned that spinning could be done by machinery for about ¾d per pound, so it is no wonder that they thought this trade was near its end. "The Population of Suffolk", said the Rainbirds, "is extremely dense for a County wholly without manufactures: I say wholly, because those at Sudbury, Lavenham, etc. are too trifling to deserve mention and, small as they are, are decreasing"[171]. In 1881 the census listed one active woolcomber, three former woolcombers and one surviving spinner of wool-yarn.

Two reminiscences, recorded as late as 1901, give us a last look at the ancient crafts of combing and spinning at Lavenham. The writer, who had lived in the town, remembered a Lavenham widow who in 1838 kept herself by spinning wool on a hand-turned wheel. He also described hand-woolcombing there in 1841. The "comb" consisted of a board to which were fixed twenty-five or thirty steel spikes, about six inches long and one inch apart; the wool was drawn again and again through the spikes. The comber bought his wool from the dealer, and when it was sufficiently combed and hanked he found his own market for it[172].

From another source it appears that each workman had two combs, which he heated in a charcoal brazier or jar. At first the wool was worked repeatedly from one comb to the other; then, to make it finer still, the wool was drawn through a comb fixed on the wall[173].

Thomas Turner is described in White's directory of 1844 as a woolstapler and yarn manufacturer, with premises in High Street.

Left: *After the Reformation the Corpus Christi Gildhall became parish property, and in the eighteenth century it was used as a Bridewell for vagrants and a workhouse for paupers.*

Below: *A horsehair loom formerly housed in the Braunche Chapel of Lavenham Church.*

Old Skills, New Materials 6

In 1769 Arthur Young had commented that rising poor rates were "miserable marks that certain Suffolk towns had the curse of manufactures among them"[174]. At first it seems strange that this man, who worked tirelessly for the modernization of agriculture, and who was living through the momentous early years of the Industrial Revolution, should be so prejudiced against manufacturing industry. But he was of course commenting not on the new inventions and processes introduced by people like Arkwright, Darby and Watt but on the older domestic industries of Suffolk, which were entering a period of mortal decline. This meant that places which had been capable of supporting fairly large populations were increasingly plagued by unemployment, low wages and poverty. By 1849 the industrial metamorphosis of Britain had gone much further, and Suffolk could be described as "wholly without manufactures"[175]. Yet this judgement was still premature so far as Lavenham was concerned.

In common with most of rural Suffolk, Lavenham's population grew at an unprecedented rate in the early part of the nineteenth century. In 1831 it stood at 2,107, the highest ever recorded, and had risen by 21% since 1778, yet the industrial importance of the town was in the meantime much reduced. Very few people still practised the old crafts, and local agriculture had been in a depressed state since the end of the Napoleonic Wars. The consequence was massive unemployment and poverty. In 1829 leading residents discussed

the possibility of financing and digging a canal to Lavenham from the River Stour at Mistley in Essex; it was seen as "the only thing to be done to save Lavenham and the neighbourhood from pauperism and ruin"; but the project never got beyond the talking stage[176].

The extent of local poverty is graphically revealed in annual returns made to Parliament[177]. In 1776 Lavenham spent £728 on poor

75

OCCUPATIONS IN LAVENHAM, 1839

[from Robson's *Directory of six counties forming the Norfolk circuit* (1839), 70]

5 bakers	1 ironmonger
1 blacksmith	2 maltsters
5 boot- & shoe-makers	1 miller
1 brazier	3 painters, plumbers & glaziers
2 bricklayers	1 rope-maker
5 butchers	2 saddlers & harness-makers
4 carpenters	4 shopkeepers
1 chemist & druggist	1 silk-throwster (Joseph Poulter)
2 coopers	1 solicitor
1 currier	3 surgeons
1 draper	3 tailors & drapers
3 farriers	8 taverns, inns and public houses
1 gig-maker	1 watch-maker
2 grocers & drapers	1 wheelwright
1 gunsmith	1 wool-manufacturer (Thos. Hitchcock)
1 hairdresser	1 wool-stapler (Turner & Son)
1 harness-maker	1 yarn-manufacturer (Wm. Meeking)

Analysis of above occupations
(those in italics are shown in more than one category)

Textiles	silk-throwster (1), wool-manufacturer (1), wool-stapler (1), yarn-manufacturer (1)	(total 4)
Leather working	currier (1), harness-maker (1), saddlers, etc. (2), *boot- and shoe-maker* (5)	(total 9)
Metal working	blacksmith (1), brazier (1), farrier (3), gunsmith (1), watchmaker (1)	(total 7)
Wood working	carpenter (4), cooper (2), gig-maker (1), wheelwright (1)	(total 8)
Other manufactures	rope-maker (1)	
Building	bricklayer (2), *carpenter* (4), painter, etc. (3)	(total 9)
Preparation of food	baker (5), butcher (5), maltster (2), miller (1)	(total 13)
Making of clothes	*boot- & shoe-maker* (5), tailor, etc. (3)	(total 8)
Retailing	draper (1), grocer, etc. (2), ironmonger (1), shopkeeper (4)	(total 8)
Other services	chemist, etc. (1), hairdresser (1), solicitor (1), surgeon (3), 'victuallers' (8)	(total 14)

relief; thereafter the costs rose sharply as the population increased, as prices were forced up during the Napoleonic Wars and as the effects of the Industrial Revolution accumulated. In 1786 the town spent £916 on relief, and in 1803 the figure jumped to £1,508. A major peak came in 1813 when no less than £2,736 had been spent. The worst year of all was 1818 when it cost £2,986 for Lavenham to relieve its poor. When the costs of relief are compared to levels of population, we see that Lavenham was in 1818 the third most impoverished parish in Suffolk; only at neighbouring Long Melford and Glemsford, where the economic problems were much the same, was the situation actually worse. Although Lavenham's annual expendi-

In the nineteenth century cottages in Church Street are known to have housed "plaiting schools" where children learned how to plait straw. Notice the large number of trees in this undated photograph.

ture on poor relief declined after that dreadful year, it still remained at over £2,000 until 1833.

The worsening economic situation induced an increasing number of people to migrate to other areas in search of work. One local example was William Mills of Lavenham, who in 1836 took his wife and six children to work for Henry Sidebottom Bros., of Houghton near Manchester[178]. As a result of this steady exodus, the total population of the town began to decline, and by 1841 had fallen to 1,871.

As the older occupations declined, certain individuals and firms introduced new industries into rural areas in the hope of giving relief and of exploiting the reserves of idle labour. In the case of Lavenham, these "replacement industries", as they have been called, also had the chance of using the redundant expertise of local people in crafts such as spinning and weaving. Although some experiments failed or were short-lived, enough new employment was generated to give Lavenham a third period of industrialization, which lasted into the twentieth century. It was sufficient to stem the outward flow of migrants so that in 1901, for the second time in its history, the recorded population of Lavenham passed 2,000.

Because, it is said, of the sharply rising cost of labour in their traditional centre at Spital-fields in London, certain silk manufacturers set up factories in East Anglia where weavers were eager for work. This industry was successfully established at Sudbury, and by 1827 it was observed that "the last exertion made in the way of manufactory [in Lavenham] was by a considerable number of weavers here being employed in weaving silk for the masters at Sudbury"[179]. We cannot quantify this information but we know that weavers were similarly employed from Long Melford and Glemsford. The "four large establishments" of Sudbury mentioned by White in his Directory of 1844 were clearly putting out work to neighbouring villages, as had the Tudor clothiers of Lavenham and their successors, the woolstaplers. Glemsford, Nayland and Lavenham soon had small silk mills of their own.

By 1839 the Lavenham firm of Joseph Poulton had its silk mill in Water Street and, under the name of Miss Mary Poulton, still existed in 1855, but it seems never to have developed into a large, thriving business. By 1847 the total number employed in silk *factories* in the whole of Suffolk was merely 606; only 108 were males, and of these fifty-five were under the age of thirteen. The Lavenham mill was later run for a few years by George

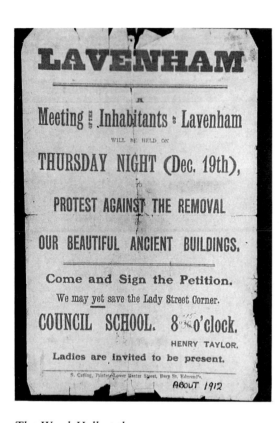

LAVENHAM

Meeting of the Inhabitants of Lavenham

WILL BE HELD ON

THURSDAY NIGHT (Dec. 19th),

to

PROTEST AGAINST THE REMOVAL

OF

OUR BEAUTIFUL ANCIENT BUILDINGS.

Come and Sign the Petition.

We may yet save the Lady Street Corner.

COUNCIL SCHOOL. 8 o'clock.

HENRY TAYLOR.

Ladies are invited to be present.

S. Catling, Printer, Lower Baxter Street, Bury St. Edmund's.

ABOUT 1912

The Wool Hall at the bottom of Lady Street was divided up into three houses and a baker's shop when the woollen industry declined in Lavenham. In 1911 it was demolished for re-erection on another site. Strong local protests backed by the Society for the Protection of Ancient Buildings led to its reprieve, and it was rebuilt on the original site by the generosity of Princess Louise, Duchess of Argyll. It subsequently became a convalescent home for railwaymen. In 1963 the building was bought by Trust Houses Limited and later incorporated into the Swan Hotel.

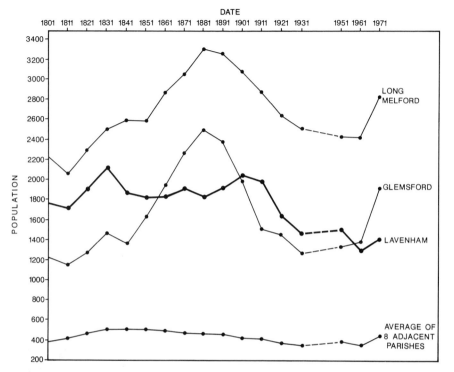

DATE
1801 1811 1821 1831 1841 1851 1861 1871 1881 1891 1901 1911 1921 1931 1951 1961 1971

A graph showing the populations of Lavenham and surrounding parishes, 1801–1971.

POPULATION

LONG MELFORD

GLEMSFORD

LAVENHAM

AVERAGE OF 8 ADJACENT PARISHES

Bentotes, but by 1868 it had ceased to weave velvets and silks and had turned to the manufacture of coconut fibre mats and matting[180].

Also in Water Street in 1844 lived Benjamin Gillingham, described as "a straw-plait and hat-manufacturer and leather-cutter". His wife and two daughters were makers of straw bonnets, and the 1851 census listed ten others in Lavenham similarly employed. However, the preparation of lengths of plait, carried on in the home, provided employment for hundreds of women and children during the greater part of the century.

This industry appears to have developed in the seventeenth century in the south-east Midlands, where by 1851 no fewer than 80% of all plaiters lived, and to have spread into Essex and Suffolk from the late-eighteenth century onwards. Splitting the selected and bleached straw with a specially designed tool, making the plait and pressing the 20-yard lengths were skilled operations. Therefore, "plaiting

schools" were established, where for a small fee quite young children learned to become efficient at the craft. Cottages in Church Street and Prentice Street are known to have housed such "schools". The finished plait was bought back by the straw dealers, and then found its way to local bonnet makers or to the hat factories of Luton. The wife of a labourer could, with sufficient skill and energy, thereby earn almost as much as her husband, to say nothing of the children's contribution. Wage-earning wives are sometimes considered a comparatively modern phenomenon, but they certainly existed in fairly large numbers in nineteenth-century Lavenham.

In 1851 a total of 300 plaiters was recorded in the parish. Although the industry continued for many years, the censuses of 1861 and 1871 each show the number reduced to about a hundred. By 1881 Lavenham had only two straw-bonnet makers, four active plaiters and two who had "formerly" plaited. The decline was in part due to the introduction of machinery into bonnet making, for which much of the hand-made plait was unsuitable. There was also strong competition from abroad, especially after 1890 when plait was imported from the Far East and the price of English plait fell sharply[181].

Meanwhile, a new "replacement industry" nearer to local traditions had arrived which was to bring back some prosperity and leave its mark on the present appearance of the town.

William Roper's factory, High Street, where horsehair was processed and coconut fibre was woven into mats and matting. This photograph was taken before the whole complex was converted into flats and given the name of Roper's Court.

White in his directory of 1855 reveals that "some of the inhabitants are now employed in weaving hair seating", and lists John Churchyard of Water Street as a "Hair seating etc. Manufacturer (also at Long Melford)". Indeed, this horsehair manufacture seems to have been brought to Melford by about 1830, and the firm must have opened its Lavenham branch between 1851 and 1855. Churchyard may have operated in both Water Street and Hall Road (in premises later destroyed), and by 1861 was employing seventy-four horsehair weavers. His son-in-law, William W. Roper, had been employed as manager at Long Melford, but by 1864 had taken over in Lavenham. He moved into larger premises

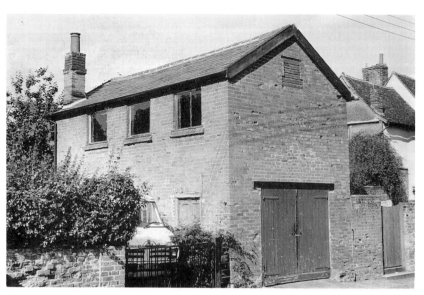

Left: *A loom-place in Hall Road. This little nineteenth-century building, now a garage, housed several horsehair looms on its two floors.*

Below left: *An advertisement by William Roper from Harrod's directory of 1864. Roper is described as "sole manufacturer" of horsehair matting for the Houses of Parliament.*

lying back from the High Street which had been vacated by the woolstapling firm of Thomas Turner. These have now been re-developed as a close of modern dwellings known as Roper's Court.

In 1871 the horsehair industry employed a total of 105 persons: eighty-three weavers, seven "servers", two "tippers", two "curlers", two "drawers", one sorter, one labourer, one carter, one loom repairer and five "factory boys". By 1881 the total of employees had risen to 203. The railway had come to Lavenham in 1865 and must have helped this growing business, which was already able to advertise itself as sole supplier to the Houses of Parliament, with an office in London. From the raw material imported from Siberia and South America the firm produced springy, curled hair for mattresses, hair for brushmaking, crinoline cloth used by tailors for padding and stiffening, kiln cloths and rough-hair cloths as well as blinds for railway carriages and ocean liners, and seating for the carriages of three railway companies[182]. Some fabric for the best upholstered furniture, or even curtains, was woven into intricate "Jacquard" designs, using hair previously dyed in a variety of colours. The dyeing was done at premises in Water

Right: *A horsehair-weaving factory built by William Roper in Water Street in 1891. It was once used as a cinema and is now converted into flats.*

Below: *Workers at Laycock's factory in Barn Street about 1900. The speciality here was horsehair seating, hence the predominance of female labour.*

Workers at Ropers' High Street factory about 1900. Here the workforce was all male, men and boys, because the product was coconut matting.

Street where, for this purpose, a natural supply of water was fed into a "canal"[183].

Ropers were by the eighteen-eighties operating three factories in the town, one in High Street and two in Water Street. In 1891 they bought the abandoned beet-sugar factory in Lower Road with the intention of manufacturing crinolines there, but it never became more than a store for their completed goods and in 1905 was almost completely destroyed by fire[184].

Besides Ropers', two other factories making horsehair seating were established in Lavenham. In 1875 the Sheffield firm of Laycocks constructed premises in Barn Street, adjoining the Grammar School which they also bought in 1890 when it finally closed. In 1908 Oddys Ltd, another firm from Sheffield, built a three-storey factory on the south-eastern outskirts of the town (now flats), where they employed forty women under a foreman[185].

The weaving of horsehair was done entirely by women in the factory or in the home, while a few men were employed as foremen or to prepare the warp, distribute hair or service the looms. In 1897 Canon Scott, the Rector of Lavenham, claimed that "every third cottage in the parish has its looms"[186]. Ropers had built and acquired many cottages, and in some cases built on "loom places" for which they charged rent; looms were also housed in garden sheds. The male preserve of preparing hair, done chiefly at the premises in High Street, involved soaking, sorting by colour and length, combing and, in the case of curled hair, bleaching with lime, washing, curling on chains and baking. Although the hair was disinfected on arrival, workers ran a risk of contracting the serious animal disease of anthrax.

Horsehair was woven on looms of

special design. The warp, which was normally between fifty and eighty yards long, was made of linen, cotton or, less commonly, silk. Because of the short length of the hair, a wooden arm called a "lath" took the place of the shuttle. Each time it moved backwards and forwards through the warp, the end of a hair was placed in a hook at its end. Canon Scott shows that a good deal of skill was required, gained only by practice,

> for the operation has to be repeated at intervals of little more than a second, and the hair has to be taken alternately from two little bundles which the weaver holds between her fingers, in one of which the thicker end of the hair is uppermost and in the other the thinner end. On an average 120 hairs go to one inch of the "seating" . . . It takes, therefore, a long time to complete the 52 yards which make up "the piece". A well-known saying in Lavenham was, "Mother will pay when she fells" [meaning when she has completed her roll of cloth and received payment]. Alas, payment was not always what one expected, for the hairs to the inch were counted and faults searched out and pennies deducted from the meagre pay[187].

William Witingham Roper had another string to his industrial bow. His extensive premises off the High Street accommodated not only the preparation of horsehair but also the manufacture of goods from coconut fibre. This was imported from Ceylon and India, and made into mats or rolls of matting. The heavy work provided employment for men, many of whose wives were meanwhile weaving horsehair. In 1861 the Census lists twelve cocofibre matmakers; in 1881 a total of thirty-three was employed, consisting of twenty-one weavers, seven "makers", four "worpers" and one winder. Thereafter this manufacture developed fast in parallel with horsehair weaving. By the first decade of the twentieth century,

This horsehair weaving factory in Brent Eleigh Road was the last to be built in the relatively prosperous days before the First World War. Erected in 1908, it has been converted into flats.

208 men and 20 boys were working at the factory in High Street[188].

The matting was woven on large iron-framed looms cast in Ipswich and furnished by local carpenters. Maintenance was done by a staff of carpenters and smiths. The fibrous yarn was dyed black, blue, red, green or orange in large vats, while white was achieved by bleaching with sulphuric acid and lime. The essential water was drawn from a well sunk to a depth of 180 feet, and pumped to the surface by a gas-powered engine. The "hard-twist" weave produced hard-wearing matting, the "back-twist" was reversible and the "plain-twist" employed a softer, less hard-wearing yarn. Finished rolls of matting were 52 yards long and varied in width from eighteen inches to six feet. The widest material required the attentions of two weavers. Quills for the shuttles were wound by apprentices with the help of a wooden machine known as a "flier". To accommodate the thick yarn, the shuttles themselves were much larger than the traditional kind and as much as fourteen inches long. With the regular handling of so much fibre, fans were needed in the factory to extract dust.

Individual mats were made by hand on frames of six different sizes. Yarn was often prepared and balled at home by children and taken to the factory in boxes on wheels known as "dillies". Demand for the mats was considerable, with orders for as many as 500 dozen being executed.

The normal working day was from 6 am to 6 pm with breaks for breakfast and lunch. On Saturdays, however, work ceased at 4 pm. One can appreciate the benefit and pleasure enjoyed by those men who were given permission to "take a harvest" in the late summer. This took them away from the factory for a few weeks, for a payment which was fixed regardless of the time spent or the weather experienced. Even in industrial Lavenham the corn harvest took precedence. It is salutary to

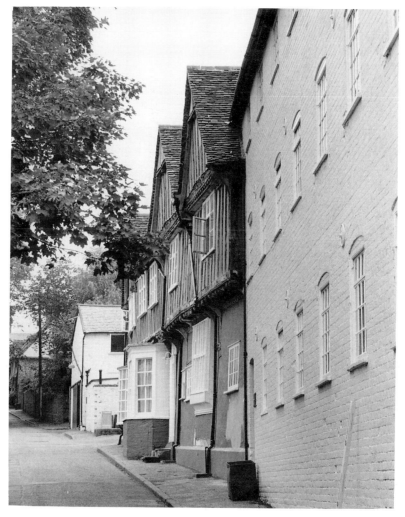

Opposite page: *The beet-sugar factory in Lower Road after the fire of 1905. Built in 1868 by James Duncan, this factory was never a commercial success and was bought in 1891 by Ropers', who used it as a store.*

Right: *The Old Grammar School in Barn Street was originally a private house but was used for educational purposes from the early seventeenth century until 1887. In 1890 the house was bought by Samuel Laycock and Sons of Sheffield, who converted the whole site into a horsehair-weaving factory.*

remember that the only holidays enjoyed at this time were bank holidays and Good Friday, which were popular times for men to work on their allotments and thereby make an important contribution to the family economy[189].

In 1868 a large new factory for producing sugar from locally grown beet was completed in Lower Road and opened by James Duncan of Mincing Lane, London. Although its product was reportedly excellent, it unfortunately was not a commercial success. It proved quite unable to compete economically with growing imports of cane sugar, and was forced to close in 1871. Another attempt was made in 1885 when the factory was reopened by Bolton and Company, but at a time when "cheap food" was increasingly imported from abroad they were no more successful than the first owners. The premises were soon closed again, and the machinery sold abroad[190]. This bold experiment, which might have helped local farmers during a period of gathering depression, was years ahead of its time. The growing and processing of beet were, in fact, successfully adopted in East Anglia in the nineteen-twenties.

Left: *Railway porters at Lavenham station handling bales of coconut mats on their way from Ropers' factory to distant customers.*

Below: *Bales of coconut fibre were stored by Ropers' in the fifteenth-century former Gildhall of Saints Peter and Paul in High Street until they were needed for weaving in the nearby factory.*

Conclusion   7

IN SPITE of the failure of the beet-sugar industry, the years from 1875 to 1914 were comparatively prosperous ones for Lavenham. Its Rector, Canon Scott, was able to observe in 1897 that with the horsehair and mat industries and the additional employment given by Baker's steam-driven roller mills and maltings, erected in the early eighteen-seventies, "it is a rare thing to find an able-bodied man or lad out of work; and to confess the truth, for a country place, spite of agricultural depression, we are fairly well-to-do"[191].

Thus Lavenham had come to terms with the modern industrial world, and its ancient streets accepted without too much disruption a handful of gaunt factories and several terraces of workers' houses. The new kinds of employment were never far removed from ancient traditions; a great deal of work was done in people's houses, and the thump of looms was still heard as it had been half a millenium earlier.

In 1904 a contributor to a local newspaper expressed surprise at finding that Lavenham was not the country village he expected. "Here", he wrote, "were all the things that go to make up a great manufacturing centre, stuck in the middle of an out-of-the-way country village, which, from its surroundings, might have been expected to be peopled with farm labourers." But he also ominously observed, "It would be a bitter day for Lavenham if either of these trades [horsehair weaving and mat-making] fall upon bad times. Work upon the land would be the only alternative for the

workers and that industry would not support a third of the population"[192].

And so, in time, it was to prove. The three horsehair businesses survived the First World War and were still functioning in 1922. But the world had changed. Markets and the supplies of raw materials had been drastically disrupted. Imports of inferior but cheaper goods now flooded the English market. Fashions in clothing and especially in upholstery abandoned the use of horsehair. Meanwhile, matting was replaced as the standard floor-covering by linoleum, which was harder wearing, cleaner and cheaper. The second generation of Ropers may have been, in the spirit of the times, more concerned to enjoy the fruits of their labour than to innovate, but

89

Left: *In celebration of an unknown jubilee, Ropers' prepared this cart to display their "World-famed Cocoa Mats and Matting" in all their many colours and patterns.*

Opposite page: *Lavenham station early this century. The line from Long Melford to Bury St Edmunds was built by the Great Eastern Railway in 1865. Above the goods shed on the left can be seen the roof of Ropers' mat factory in High Street.*

Lower left: *The cowls of malt kilns are prominent in this photograph of Lady Street about 1900. The fine medieval house in the foreground was later demolished and re-erected at Walberswick.*

in the face of a world-wide economic depression this was no time to embark on new large-scale ventures. By 1930 the Ropers' business had failed, and the factories of Oddy and Laycock had also closed. Much unemployment resulted and the population fell to 1,400 in 1931. After at least 600 years, and probably much longer, from broadcloth to horsehair seating, Lavenham's great tradition of weaving eventually died, and the town slept.

Yet even today, famous as it has now become as a resort for tourists and antiquarians, Lavenham is not without its industries. A cosmetics factory now occupies premises on the site of the old sugar factory and on the former railway sidings abandoned when Lavenham's station was finally closed in the nineteen-sixties; a small metal-pressing works occupies the old grammar school and its adjacent factory; while a printing and publishing business operates in Water Street in premises once occupied by a horsehair weaving firm. Embedded in the picturesque and largely residential streets of today, this modest survival of industrial enterprise is a precious link with the past which still to some extent keeps Lavenham "a working village". It reminds us that Lavenham is not so much a classic village as the beautiful fossilization of a vanished age when industry had a more domestic and more human scale.

If Lavenham's industry had reached its zenith not in the fifteen-twenties but in the age of the factory system, or, to put it another way, if the many craftsmen employed by Thomas Spring III had been set to work in the same building or complex, and other factories had housed the employees of the Risbys, the Sextens, the Gromes and the Huntes, and if steam power had driven their looms and spinning machines, what a "dark, Satanic" aspect the town might now have worn!

References

Abbreviations

BL	British Library
BPP	*British Parliamentary Papers*
CUL	Cambridge University Library
HMC	Historical Manuscripts Commission
L & P Hen. VIII	*Letters & Papers of the Reign of Henry VIII*
NNRO	Norfolk and Norwich Record Office
PCC	Prerogative Court of Canterbury
Pound	John Pound (ed.), *The Military Survey of 1522 for Babergh Hundred*, Suffolk Records Society, XXVIII (1986)
PRO	Public Record Office, London
PSIA	*Proceedings of the Suffolk Institute of Archaeology and History*
SP Dom.	State Papers, Domestic (PRO)
SRO(B)	Suffolk Record Office, Bury St Edmunds branch
VCH	*Victoria County History*

1. Roggerus Fullo de Lafham, mentioned in R. H. C. Davis (ed.), *Kalendar of Abbot Samson*, Camden 3rd Series, LXXXIV (1954), 59; Davis interprets Lafham as Lavenham, but it was undoubtedly a hamlet of Hadleigh (see *PSIA*, XXVIII, 101).

2. *Suffolk in 1327: Subsidy Return*, Suffolk Green Books, no IX, vol. 11 (1906).

3. Other sources indicate that Sudbury cloth was produced for export *via* Ipswich by the late thirteenth century, and that in 1305 the manor of the Archbishop of Canterbury at Hadleigh contained four fullers, one fulling mill and a dyehouse (see *VCH, Suffolk*, II, 255; *PSIA*, XI, 152-172).

4. One occupation, that of fuller, was very poorly represented in the area, with only two examples out of twenty-eight. In fact, most of the people bearing the name of Fuller in 1327 seem to have been scattered in the centre and north of the county. This is curious, as one of the usual explanations of the development of the cloth industry in southern East Anglia is the suitability of its streams and rivers for the newly-invented fulling mills. Certainly such mills were working in the Babergh–Cosford area by the early years of the fourteenth century (see Note 79). The explanation may simply be that some fullers are hidden under such names as le Mellere, le Melne and atte Melne (*Melne* means mill); indeed those names, which must include ordinary corn millers, occurred fifty-five times in Suffolk, and fourteen of them (25.5%) were within Babergh and Cosford. This is much more like the proportion one would expect.

5. Thomas Fuller (1608–1661) appears to have been the origin of this myth. He wrote that before 1337 "English men knew no more what to do with their wool than the sheep that wore it". Canon Scott in his *Visitor's Guide to Lavenham* (1897) was one of those who applied Fuller's interpretation to Lavenham (pp. 7-8), and it has unfortunately stuck. For a general discussion of Edward III's decision, see May McKisack, *The Fourteenth Century, 1307–99* (1959), 367-368.

6. Thomas Fuller, *The History of the Worthies of England*, (1662), p. 279: "It is enough for Northamptonshire to sell their Wooll, whilst that other Countrys make cloth thereof. . . ."

7. Blackwell Hall, a large and ancient building on the east side of the Guildhall, in the City of London, was in 1386 converted by the corporation to a warehouse and market place for all sorts of woollen cloth brought from all parts of the country. By an Act of the Common Council dated 8th August, 1516, this was to be

the only market in London for such woollen manufactures. The Hall no longer stands (see Hatton's *New View of London* (1708), 599).

8. Joan Thirsk, "Industries in the Countryside" in F. J. Fisher (ed.), *Essays in the Economic and Social History of Tudor and Stuart England* (1961), 70-88.

9. Joan Thirsk, *ibid.*, 74-75.

10. Will of John Place, 1440: SRO(B), 24 Baldwyne; will of John Harry, 1473: SRO(B), 536 Baldwyne.

11. Lavenham's charter for a weekly market on Tuesdays was granted in 1257 by Henry III to Hugh de Vere, Earl of Oxford, and a further charter of 1329 allowed Robert de Vere's manorial tenants to pass quit of toll throughout England (*Cal. Charter Rolls*, I, 475; IV, 122).

12. BL, Harl. 98, f. 152.

13. Norman Scarfe, *The Suffolk Landscape* (1972), 166, Fig. 13.

14. *Cal. Patent Rolls, Edward III, 1358–61*, 139.

15. *Cal. Patent Rolls, Richard II, 1396–99*, 178–182; W. Cunningham, *The Growth of English Industry and Commerce* (5th edn 1915), 385n.

16. *Cal. Patent Rolls* covering years 1390–1420.

17. PRO, E101/342/8, 10.

18. Pound, pp. 75-87.

19. *Household Book of Dame Alice de Bryene, 1412–13* (Suffolk Institute of Archaeology, 1931), 120.

20. Gladys Thornton, *A History of Clare, Suffolk* (1928), 148-149.

20a. In fact, John Brampton and Roger Grome registered large totals of 113 and 110 cloths respectively, yet they each appeared only once.

20b. The relevant aulnage accounts will be found in the PRO as follows: E101/342/21; E101/342/24; E101/342/25; E101/343/2; E101/343/5 and E101/343/7. For a useful comparison within East Anglia in the same period, see R. H. Britnell, *Growth and Decline in Colchester, 1300–1525* (1986).

21. Sir William Parker, *History of Long Melford* (1873), 70-73, 77-87.

22. Will of 13th Earl of Oxford, 1513: PRO, PCC, 11 Fettiplace.

23. Will of William Jacob, 1500: NNRO, 115/6 Cage; will of Elizabeth Braunche, 1502: PRO, PCC, 11 Blamyr; will of John Newton, 1502: PRO, PCC, 20 Blamyr.
(The mark was not an English coin, but was often used as a unit of accounting. It was a weight of metal originally valued at 128 silver pennies, that is 10s 8d, but later revalued at 13s 4d.)

24. Will of John Risby, 1504: PRO, PCC, 20 Holgrave.

25. Will of Symond Causton, 1521: PRO, PCC, 7 Maynwaryng.

26. Manuscripts of the Corporation of Eye, in *HMC Report*, X (4), 531-532.

27. During the century before 1485, a total of £140 was bequeathed to the fabric of Lavenham church by forty donors, at least nine of whom are known to have been connected with the cloth trade. This was presumably spent on the maintenance of the old building, of which the chancel still survives.

28. Pound, p. 80 for John Roger and Robert King, p. 78 for William Galaunte, and p. 81 for John Grace, who was of "no substance".

29. John Harvey, *The Perpendicular Style* (1978), 217, 230: Harvey writes of the development of enriched spandrels in nave arcading with a substantial horizontal "frieze" above them. This feature was taken up by John Wastell, "to whom all the major East Anglian examples are attributed upon very strong evidence by Mr Oswald: Great St Mary's, Cambridge (1491), Lavenham (1495) and Saffron Walden (1497)". It is to Simon Clerk that Arthur Oswald attributed Lavenham's tower (1486–1525) with its "panelled, clasping buttresses against which are applied pairs of set-back buttresses, in the same manner as the buttresses on each side of the west porch at Westminster Abbey".

30. Will of Thomas Sexten, 1529: PRO, PCC, 15 Jankyn; will of Robert Critofte, 1539: PRO, PCC, 27 Dyngeley.

31. Will of Symond Causton, 1521: PRO, PCC, 7 Maynwaryng. William Causton is described in the 1524 Lay Subsidy as "at cross"; he is further described as "dwelling by the cross in Lavenham" in the will of Margaret Rysby, 1552: PRO, PCC, 4 Tashe. Will of Thomas Causton, 1624: SRO(B), 27 Pearle.

32. Will of John Whatlock, 1558: PRO, PCC, 28 Noodes.

33. Will of John Newton, 1544: SRO(B), 454 Longe. Members of the Newton family were subsequently involved in a dispute over property which included "one great messuage called the Swan" (PRO, REQ 2, XXIV, 13).

34. For example, Little Hall, The Priory, 10 Church Street, 98-100 High Street, Barn Cottage, Woolstaplers in Prentice Street, 19 Shilling Street and 7 Lady Street; 90 Church Street is a medieval house of "Wealden" type; 88 High Street is a half-aisled medieval house.

35. For example, The Willows, Fir Tree House, 91-94 High Street, 1-5 High Street, 19-21 High Street, 42-44 High Street, Hilmorton House in High Street and Arundel House in Shilling Street; Shilling Grange is an instructive example because half its facade is still Georgian and the other half is drastically restored timber-framing.

36. Examples of first-floor doors survive at 30 and 67 Water Street, Brett House in Prentice Street, and 15 Market Place. Pargeted emblems are to be seen on Blaize House in Church Street, the Swan Hotel and The Priory in Water Street. For good details about the interiors of houses, see F. Lingard Ranson, *Lavenham, Suffolk* (1937 and subsequent editions).

37. For example, in 1456 Robert Jolly, butcher, bequeathed to John Joly "the stall in the Market of Lavenham between the stall of Robert Joly his father on the one side and the Market House on the other" (NNRO, 30 Neve); Robert Welymet in 1502 left to his wife Elizabeth "my tenement in the Market lying between the tenement of Roger Gryn on the one part and the tollhouse of the Earl of Oxford on the other part" (Canterbury Archives, *sede vacante*, Reg. F, f. 263).

38. Will of William Jacob, 1500: NNRO, 115 Cage.

39. See for example Canon Scott, *The Visitor's Guide to Lavenham* (1897), 37.

40. F. E. Warren, "A Pre-Reformation Village Gild", *PSIA*, XI, 81-134; other account books survive for gilds at Creeting, Suffolk (PRO, E 135, 2/22) and at Lt Walsingham, Norfolk (PRO, E 101/517/28).

41. For example, will of Robert Parson, 1478: SRO(B), 178 Hervye; will of Myles Wytton, 1520 PRO, PCC, 6 Maynwaryng.

42. In 1501 Elizabeth Braunche left a tenement to the Gild of the Holy Trinity, only if the named beneficiary neglected an annual payment of 10s for her "yeartide": PRO, PCC, 11 Blamyr.

43. *Cal. Patent Rolls, Edward VI, 1548–49*, 79-80.

44. Will of John Rysby, 1493: PRO, PCC, 25 Dogett.

45. *Cal. Patent Rolls, Henry VII, 1494–1509*, 572.

46. Will of John Barker, 1544: PRO, PCC, 17 Pynnyng.

47. Debts of Thomas Spring III in Pound, p. 75.

48. Debts of John Barker, 1609, in J. E. Pilgrim, "The Cloth Industry in Essex and Suffolk, 1558–1640", MA thesis, Univ. of London (1940), p. 13.

49. Ledger of Thomas Howell, 1519–27, library of Drapers' Hall, London.

50. Will of John Pinchbeck, 1648: SRO(B), 35 Ashton.

51. Will of Thomas Braunche, 1499: PRO, PCC, 32 Horne.

52. PRO, C1/449/6; C1/1489/115.

53. *Household Book of Dame Alice de Bryene, 1412–13* (Suffolk Institute of Archaeology, 1931), 117.

54. A. R. Myers (ed.), *English Historical Documents*, IV, 1028-1029.

55. Peter J. Bowden, *The Wool Trade in Tudor and Stuart England* (1962), 64.

56. Will of Roger Reve, 1538: PRO, PCC, 24 Dyngeley.

57. BL, Cott. MS, Titus, B. v, f. 254; *State Papers, Foreign, 1560–61*, p. 524, no 942 (Jan., 1561).

58. Will of John Hunte, 1539: PRO, PCC, 6 Alenger; will of Robert Grome, 1540: PRO, PCC, 16 Alenger; will of John Grome, 1587: PRO, PCC, 75 Spencer.

59. Ledger of Thomas Kytson: CUL, Hengrave MSS, 78.

60. Will of Thomas Sturmyne, 1493: PRO, PCC, 3 Vox.

61. Inventory of Thomas Goodridge, 1668: SRO(B), IC 500/3/13 (173).

62. *VCH, Suffolk*, II, 258, quoting SP Dom. Eliz. cxiv, 32.

63. BL, Add. MS 39245, f. 65.

64. P. Stockham (ed.), *The Book of Trades* (1976 reprint of American edn of 1807, based on English edn of 1804), 9.

65. *VCH, Suffolk*, II, 259, quoting *L & P Hen. VIII*, XIV (1), 874.

66. "The Pleasant History of John Winchcombe" in F. O. Mann (ed.), *The Works of Thomas Deloney* (1912), 20.

67. "Ordinances for the reformation of abuses in the craft of the weavers", 8th June, 1477, among manuscripts of the Corporation of Bury St Edmunds, in *HMC Report*, XIV (8), 133-138.

68. Will of John Bolton, 1440: SRO(B), 59 Baldwyne.

69. PRO, E 159/403, 181.

70. John Webb, *Great Tooley of Ipswich* (1962), 101, quoting Early Chancery Proceedings, PRO, 627/20.

71. Will of Thomas Spring III, 1523: PRO, PCC, 11 Bodfelde (see Appendix 1).

72. For debts of John Barker, 1609, see Note 42.

73. Inventory of William Spryng, 1476: PRO, PCC, PROB 2/7.

74. BL, Cott. MS, Titus, B.v. f. 254.

75. Aulnage accounts of 1434–35: PRO, E 101/342/23.

76. Will of John Ponder, 1520: PRO, PCC, 30 Ayloffe.

77. Record Commissioners, *Nonarum Inquisitiones* (1807), 103, *sub* Waldyngfeld Magna.

78. For general information on dyeing, see William Partridge, *A Practical Treatise on Dying* (1828, reprinted 1973); Barrie Trinder and Jeff Cox, *Yeomen and Colliers in Telford* (1980), 47-61.

79. Will of Roger Grome, 1562: PRO, PCC, 18 Streat; will of Roger Ruggle (or Rogell), 1580: PRO, PCC, 24 Watson; will of William Grome, senior, 1553: PRO, PCC, 22 More.

80. A brick-built culvert beneath Water Street has been recently explored (1987). It has side-branches under High Street and Lady Street. The brickwork of the culvert under the Priory appears to be fifteenth century. It would be surprising if this major investment had no more than domestic significance and no connection with the burgeoning industry of the late-medieval town.

81. Map of Long Melford, 1580, in possession of Sir Richard Hyde Parker; printed by Long Melford Historical and Archaeological Society, Occasional Publication no 1, *Israel Amyce's Map of Melford Manor, 1580* (?1986).

82. Will of Roger Crytott, 1476: SRO(B), 52 Hervey; will of John Carpenter, 1416: NNRO, 18/19 Hyrnyng.

83. Will of Thomas Wyllymott, 1460: SRO(B), 304 Baldwyne; will of Robert Wyllymott, 1502: Canterbury Cathedral Archives, *sede vacante*, F, f. 263; will of Elizabeth Wyllymott, 1504: PRO, PCC, 19 Holgrave.

84. Will of John Fermer, 1523: PRO, PCC, 16 Bodfelde.

85. Lord John Hervey, "Extent of Hadleigh Manor, 1305", *PSIA*, XI (1903), 152; G. A. Thornton, *A History of Clare, Suffolk* (1928), 20, 187; S. H. A. Hervey, *Gt and Lt Whelnetham Parish Register*, Suffolk Green Books, XV (1910), 292 (for Flatford); *Cal. Ancient Deeds*, II, A 3510 (for Hintlesham), A 3778

(Nayland); *Valor Ecclesiasticus*, III, 415 (Dedham, Essex). The Lark valley in north-west Suffolk had a cluster of medieval fulling mills: see SRO(B), E 3/15.6/2.1b (Fornham); SRO(B), 449/2/566 (West Stow); SRO(B), 449/2/366 (Lackford); *Cal. Inquisitions Post Mortem*, XVI, 7-15 Rich. II, p. 164 (Cavenham); Antonia Gransden (ed.), *Letter Book of William of Hoo . . . 1280–94* (1963), p. 122 (Icklingham).

86. Will of John Lymmour, 1528: PRO, PCC, 2 Jankyn; will of Roger Grome, 1539: SRO(B), 301 Longe.

87. Bourne Mill is a National Trust property lying one mile south of Colchester. It is said to have been built c1591 as a fishing lodge and later converted into a mill. See Hervey Benham, *Some Essex Water Mills* (1976), 21-24, 96-97.

88. Will of Thomas Sexten, 1529: PRO, PCC, 15(23) Jankyn.

89. A. Betterton, "A Survival from Lavenham's Cloth Industry", *PSIA*, XXXV, Pt 4 (1984), 317-319.

90. *Ex inf*. Alan and Gwynneth Casey.

91. Will of John Browne, 1542: SRO(B), 27 Colman; will of Edmund Matthyman, 1559; SRO(B), 43 Woode; will of Thomas Hamond, 1589: SRO(B), 272 Goddarde; will of Richard Hurrell, 1615: SRO(B), 369 Steven; will of John Kinge, 1597: SRO(B), 303 Blomfielde.

92. Record Commissioners, *Nonarum Inquisitiones* (1807), 103 (Long Melford), 104 (Glemsford).

93. *Rolls of Parliament*, V (1439–68), 629-630.

94. Aulnage accounts: PRO, E 101/343/2.

95. *Statutes of the Realm*, IV (1), 136-141.

96. Will of William Rysby, 1506: PRO, PCC, 12 Adeane.

97. Pound, pp. 75-82; *Suffolk in 1524: Subsidy Return*, Suffolk Green Books, no X (1910), pp. 24-29.

98. J. Patten, "Village and Town: an Occupational Study", *Agric. Hist. Review*, 20 (1972), 1-16.

99. J. Patten, *ibid.*, 9, Table II, estimates that the population of Lavenham in 1522 was 1,050. By 1603 he puts the figure at 1,200, rising to 1,500 in 1670: J. Patten, *English Towns, 1500–1700* (1978), 251. The Chantry Certificate of 1546 asserted that "Lavenham has 2,000 people", surely an exaggeration: *PSIA*, XII, 31. Peter Laslett's work on one hundred communities in pre-industrial England suggests an average household size of 4.75: Peter Laslett & Richard Wall, *Household and Family in Past Time* (1972), 125-158.

100. J. Ambrose Raftis, *Warboys* (1974), 147-150.

101. *Cal. Patent Rolls, Henry VI, 1429–36*, 558, 565.

102. W. G. Hoskins, *Local History in England* (1972), Appendix 1, 239.

103. Barbara McClenaghan, *The Springs of Lavenham* (1924), Appendix D, 86-88.

104. W. G. Hoskins, "English Provincial Towns in the Early 16th Century" in *Provincial England* (1965), 73-74.

105. David Dymond, "The Famine of 1527 in Essex", *Local Population Studies*, no 26 (1981), 34-39.

106. John Webb, *Great Tooley of Ipswich* (1962), 86, 101.

107. Edward Hall, *Chronicle* (1809 edn), 699-700.

108. *L & P Hen. VIII*, IV (1), 1329.

109. *L & P Hen. VIII*, IV (1), 1323, 1343.

110. *L & P Hen. VIII*, IV (2), 3703.

111. *L & P Hen. VIII*, IV (2), 4012, 4044, 4239; *VCH, Suffolk*, II, 257.

112. *L & P Hen. VIII*, IV (2), 4282.

113. *L & P Hen. VIII*, XI, 625, 626, 642.

114. *Statutes of the Realm*, IV (1), 136-141.

115. *Ibid*, IV (1), 141-142.

116. *Acts of the Privy Council*, June 1630–June 1631, no 1017, 342-343.

117. *Cal. Patent Rolls*, Edward VI, 1553, 9-10; Philip & Mary, 1553–54, 386; Philip & Mary, 1554–55, 266-267.

128. R. H. Tawney & E. Power (eds), *Tudor Economic Documents*, III, 210-225.

129. G. D. Ramsay, "The Distribution of the Cloth Industry in 1561–2", *English Hist. Review*, LVII (1942), 361-369.

130. *Suffolk in 1568: Subsidy Return*, Suffolk Green Books, no XII, 6-7.

131. One of the two wealthiest men in Suffolk in 1568 was Sir Thomas Kitson of Hengrave, whose father had prospered as a merchant sending ships to the Continent. Surviving accounts list cargoes of cloth, but unfortunately appear not to mention Lavenham (Cambridge University Library: Hengrave MSS, 78, 1-4).

132. W. G. Hoskins, *Provincial England* (1965), 74-76.

133. John Nicholls, *The Progresses of Queen Elizabeth I* (1788) II, 52.

134. G.E.C., *Complete Baronetage*, II (1902), 129-130; A. Wagner, *English Genealogy* (1972), 162.

135. William Harrison, *The Description of England* (ed. Georges Edelen, for Folger Shakespeare Library, 1968), 309.

136. L. F. Salzman, *English Industries of the Middle Ages* (1923), 243-244; Eric Kerridge, "Wool Growing and Wool Textiles in Medieval and Early Modern Times", in J. Geraint Jenkins (ed.), *The Wool Textile Industry in Great Britain* (1972); Eric Kerridge, *Textile Manufacturers in Early Modern England* (1985).

137. J. E. Pilgrim, "The Cloth Industry in East Anglia" in J. Geraint Jenkins (ed.), *ibid.* (1972), 256.

138. In C. Singer *et al.*, *A History of Technology*, III, 178, it is pointed out that the nature of many cloths changed with time, and that imitations assumed false designations.

139. For example, Van Eyck's "Jan Arnolfini and his Wife" in the National Gallery, contrasted with Elizabethan portraits by Nicholas Hillyard and Isaac Oliver or with Van Dyck's early Stuart studies.

130. D. C. Coleman, "An Innovation and its Diffusion: the New Draperies", *Econ. Hist. Review*, 2nd Series, 22 (1969), 417-429.

131. Daniel Defoe, *A Tour through the Whole Island of Great Britain* (intro. by G. D. H. Cole, 1927) I, 48.

132. *VCH, Suffolk*, II, 267, quoting SP Dom. Eliz. CXIV, 32.

133. T. W. Oswald Hicks, *A Calendar of Wills relating to . . . Suffolk* (PCC, 1383–1604) (1913), 28-30.

134. PRO: E 159/403, 181; 436, 217.

135. PRO: SP Dom. Eliz. 271, no 15; 273, no 30.

136. J. E. Pilgrim, "The Cloth Industry in Essex and Suffolk, 1558–1640", MA thesis, University of London (1940), 137.

137. SRO (B), D9/1, Part a, m.5.

138. Letter Book of the Deputy Lieutenants and JPs of Suffolk: *HMC Report*, XIII, Appendix IV, 439-440.

139. Warrant to churchwardens and overseers, 20th Nov. 1622: BL, Add. 39245.

140. G. D. Ramsay, "The Report of the Royal Commission on the Clothing Industry, 1640", *English Hist. Review*, LVII (1942), 482-493.

141. *HMC Report*, XIII, Appendix IV, 440.

142. Will of Thomas Taylor, 1625: SRO(B), 278 Pearle; will of Ambrose Pricke, 1631: SRO(B), 60 Colman.

143. Richard Blome, *Britannia* (1673), 208, 211-212. An estimate based on parish registers indicates that in about 1670 Lavenham's population reached a peak: it may have stood as high as about 1,900 inhabitants, though Patten suggested 1,500 (see notes 98 and 99).

144. Probate inventory of Edward Beare, 1680: SRO(B), IC 500/3/20 (220).

145. *Suffolk in 1674: the Hearth Tax*, Suffolk Green Books, no XI, vol. 13, 187-190. The figure of 52.4% represents those exempted from payment of tax on the grounds of poverty.

146. Probate inventory of Thomas Goodridge, 1668: SRO(B), IC 500/3/13 (173); probate inventory of Nicholas Wells, 1667: NNRO, INV 55/118; probate inventory of William Wiles, senior, 1666: SRO(B), IC 500/3/12 (30).

147. Probate inventory of Francis Cannum, 1669: SRO(B), IC 500/3/14 (101).

148. Probate inventory of Edward Millman, 1682: SRO(B), IC 500/3/21 (160).

149. Probate inventory of Richard Palmer, 1667: SRO(B), IC 500/3/12 (92); Henry Witheat in 1696 had "Brazil skins": SRO(B), IC 500/3/25 (12).

150. SRO(B), Acc. 1531/7/1/3.

151. BL, Harl. 98, f. 152.

152. F. Grace, "The Population of East Bergholt, 1653–1836 . . .", *Suffolk Review*, 3 (8) (1970), 260-272.

153. Parish register, baptisms 1753–1809 and burials 1757–1809: SRO(B), FL 508/4/4.

154. Robert Reyce's "Breviary of Suffolk" in Lord Francis Hervey (ed.), *Suffolk in the XVIIth Century* (1902), 22-23.

155. Ephraim Chambers, *Cyclopaedia or Universal Dictionary of Arts and Science*, II (1738), *sub* "Woollen manufactory".

156. Thomas Cox, *Magna Britannia*, V (1730), 176-179.

157. Travels of Dr Richard Pococke, 1764: BL, Add. 14260.

158. Josiah Gilbert (ed.), *Autobiography and Other Memorials of Mrs Gilbert (formerly Ann Taylor)* (1878), 39-40.

159. Will of William Causton, 1633: SRO(B), 298 Colman.

160. Deeds of Fir Tree House, Lavenham: SRO(B), Acc. 2373/1-3; Acc. 2375.

161. Josiah Gilbert (ed.), *op. cit.* (1878), 19, 31, 58.

162. Abstracts of the Returns of Overseers, *Sessional Papers*, 31 (1777), 165.

163. Apprenticeship indentures: SRO(B), 1531/7/7 (1-125).

164. See W. E. Tate, *The Parish Chest* (1960), 220-225.

165. Register of burials: SRO(B), FL 508/4 Order book of Suffolk Quarter Sessio SRO(I), 105/2/11, ff. 74-75.

165a. *Bury & Norwich Post*, 6th March, 1793.

166. A. Young, *General View of the Agriculture Suffolk* (1813), 231; Frederic Shoberl, *? Beauties of England and Wales*, XIV (181 152.

167. *VCH, Suffolk*, II, 270; A Young, *Six Wee Tour* (1769), 63.

168. *Bury & Norwich Post*, 9 Feb. 1825.

169. Robson's *Directory of Six Counties form the Norfolk Circuit* (1839), 70, gives a use classification of Lavenham's trades; Willi White, *Directory of Suffolk* (1844), 553-55

170. *BPP*, 1843, XII.

171. William and Hugh Rainbird, *Agriculture Suffolk* (1849), 281.

172. *East Anglian Miscellany* (1901, reprin 1965), 1901, nos 126 & 135.

173. P. Stockham (ed.), *The Book of Tra* (reprint 1976 of American edn of 1807, bas on English edn of 1804), 1-7.

174. A. Young, *Eastern Tour* (1771), IV, 360-3

175. William and Hugh Rainbird, *op. cit.* (184 281.

176. *Bury & Norwich Post*, 18 Feb. 1829.

177. Abstracts of Returns made by Oversee 1776, in *Sessional Papers*, vol. 31; returns 1803 in *BPP*, 1803–4, XIII; returns of 1813 in *BPP*, 1818, XIX; returns of 1816–21 *BPP*, 1822, V; returns for 1822–24 in *B* 1825, IV; returns of 1825–29 in *BPP*, 1830 XL; returns of 1830–34 in *BPP*, 1835, LV

178. *BPP*, 1843, XLV.

179. Anon., *A Concise Description of Bury Edmunds and its Environs* (1827).

180. Robson's *Directory of Six Counties* . (1839), 70; William White, *Directory of S folk* (1855), 756, 758; Morris & Co., *Direct of Suffolk* (1868), 327.

181. Enumerators' books for censuses of 18 1861, 1871 and 1881, for which microfilms available in SRO(B); *VCH, Suffolk*, II, 2

254; H. E Fitzrandolph & M. P. Hay, *The Rural Industries of England and Wales*, II (1926, reprinted 1977), 119-120; III (1927, reprinted 1978), 97-98.

. Harrod's *Directory of Suffolk* (1864), among advertisements at back; William White, *Directory of Suffolk* (1885), 453, 456.

. This was undoubtedly the site where Roger Ruggle dyed his wool in the sixteenth century (see pp. 33–34).

. F. Lingard Ranson, *Lavenham, Suffolk* (1937), 17.

High Street in the nineteen-twenties, with motor transport beginning to have its effect; note the garage on the left. Other modern facilities include the gas lamp and the obtrusive telegraph poles. Compare the photograph on page 51, taken from almost the same viewpoint perhaps half a century earlier.

185. William White, *Directory of Suffolk* (1891–2), 506-509; Kelly's *Directory of Suffolk* (1908), 284.

186. Canon Scott, *The Visitor's Guide to Lavenham and its Church* (1897), 9.

187. Canon Scott, *ibid.*, 43-44.

188. *Ex inf.* Mrs Margaret Turner of Lavenham.

189. *Ex inf.* Mrs Margaret Turner; *Bury & Norwich Post and Suffolk Standard*, 1 Nov. 1904, 6; *VCH, Suffolk*, II, 275–276; Canon Scott, *ibid.*, 9.

190. F. Lingard Ranson, *ibid.*, 17; *Journal Royal Agric. Soc.*, 3rd series, IX (1898), 344-346..

191. Canon Scott, *ibid.*, 10.

192. *Bury & Norwich Post and Suffolk Standard*, 1 Nov. 1904, 6.

Accounts of Executors of Thomas Spring III (?1523–24)

PRO: PROB 2/14

(Translated from Latin; square brackets are used where the writing is illegible or missing, and roun brackets where the original Latin is given.)

[First section illegible]

And paid to John Spring, the elder, son of the said testator, as a legacy .... £2(

And paid to Frances, daughter of the same John Spring, to whom the said testator gave an bequeathed.. 100 mar▮

And paid to Robert Spring, son of the said testator, as a legacy...£4⁴

And paid to the fifteen children (pueris) of Thomas Jermyn, namely to each of them now living, as legacy [ ] £20...£3(

And paid as a gift and legacy of the said testator to each of the children (puerorum) of Rose Guybon no surviving £20 ....£€

And paid to the daughter of the said testator's wife begotten (Genite) by her first husband as the gift an legacy of the same testator when she reaches the age of sixteen ....£26. 13.

And paid each of the boys whom the same testator raised from the holy font[1] (levavit de sacrofonte) as legacy 3s 4d ....[

And paid among the domestic servants (inter famulos domesticos) as a gift and legacy of the said testator, ▮ be divided among them equally according to the discretion of his executors...........................£59. 0.

And paid to the Bailiff of Lavenham, William Bertryn, as a legacy ....£1(

And paid to Peter Gauge [ ] of the said testator, as a gift and legacy of the same testator, ten half-balls ◀ woad (decem half ball' wode) valued in the inventory ....£▮

And paid to the repairs of roads lying around the township (villam) of Lavenham, where they shall see▮ necessary to the executors... 100 mar▮

And paid to Sir William Waldegrave as a legacy of the said testator .... 100 mar▮

And paid by the said executors for [ ] of one new tomb on the grave of the said deceased (unius no▼ Tumbe super tumulum dicti defuncti) according to the form of the testament, with a parclose about t▮ same (cum parclusorio circum eundem).. 100 mar▮

And paid to the repair of roads lying within the boundaries of the township (in circuitu ville) of Lavenhar▮ beyond the 100 marks bequeathed by the said testator in his will for the repair of similar road distributed by the said Master Jermyn .... 100 mar▮

SUM OF LEGACIES PAID   £3,401. 2. 8

Paid by the said executors for the support of scholars studying in the universities of Cambridge and Oxfo▮ (pro exhibitione Scholarum in universitatibus Cant' & oxon' student'), for the soul of the sa▮ deceased .... 100 mar▮

paid by the same executors in alms among poor people (in Elemosina inter pauperes) both within t▮ township of Lavenham and in divers townships in the district (in patria), by the discretion of the sa▮ Thomas Jermyn and William Waldegrave, as by a certain book of particulars of the same executors € this [ ] with £35. 2. 5 spent on the Anniversary day.

And paid for the repair of roads lying within the boundaries of the township of Lavenham, beyond t▮ 100 marks bequeathed by the said deceased in the will as above, and distributed by the said Thom▮ Jermyn .... 100 mar▮

In moneys (denariis) expended on the raising of the bell-tower and chapel founded within Lavenham church (super exaltacione Campanilis & Capelle Fundat' infra ecclesiam de laneham), by the discretion of the said executors, beyond and except the £200 bequeathed in the will of the said testator for the building (reparacionem) of the same bell-tower, as appears above among the legacies £479. 15. 4

SUM   £893. 9. 5

Paid to the Lord King as moneys lent(?) (mutuat') to him, by reason of the portion of 500 marks bequeathed by the said testator to his youngest daughter, Bridget, and remaining in the custody of the said executor on account of the minority of the same Bridget (ratione minoris etatis eiusdem Brigitte) £16. 13. 4

SUM   £16. 13. 4

For moneys spent by the said executors between the wife, children and friends (inter uxorem liberos & amicos) gathered together in the house of the said deceased at Lavenham, at the time of the division and distribution of stock and domestic items, divided among them, according to the will of the same testator ....28s. 1d.

In divers other expences paid by them, on account of the divers legacies given to divers persons by the said testator, living in the district in divers townships, and sent to them by the same executors.... 10s.4d.

To John Hunt and William Undon, Burgesses of the town of Lavenham, for attending the Parliament held in London (Compentibus ad parliamentum tentum london [sic]) in the 14th year of King Henry VIII, for their expenses .... 13s.4d.

To Thomas Sporne, keeper of the King's seal, for affixing the same seal to 411 saleable cloths of the said testator (pro Appositione eiusdem sigilli ad iiij^{c}xj pannos venales)..£6. 17. 0

And also for expenses given to John Syday for divers tasks done by him (pro diversis laboribus per ipsum factis), as reckoned in the particulars, and there remains £4. 13. 4

[last four items] in all £12. 14. 0

SUM   £14. 2. 1

And paid for the expenses of the said Thomas Jermyn, executor, appearing twice in the prerogative court on two citations, with other expenses for retaining counsel in the spiritual court in the causes and business of the said testator, that is, in riding from his house in the county of Suffolk to London and there staying for four weeks, with four horses and as many servants and [ ], as appears through the particulars noted in a certain schedule (bills)..£10

SUM   £10

SUM OF ALL THE AFORESAID ALLOWANCES (ALLOUUM) AND PAYMENTS £5,500. 9. 4

AND THERE REMAINS   £2,592. 2. 5   From which is allocated 60s. for the fees of the commissary (3s.4d.) and of the Auditors (40s.) together with the general discharge 6s.8d. (Acquietanc' Generali) with other expenses [ ]

AND THERE REMAINS BEYOND   £2,589. 2. 5
FROM WHICH

[ ] by the aforesaid executors £200, which they assert to have paid for lands [ ] annual value of 20 marks for a certain chantry to be founded within Lavenham church, in which it is ordained that two competent (honest') chaplains may celebrate mass, and six poor men pray there each day for evermore (quod duo capellani honesti celebra—, & sex pauperes ibidem cotidie imperpetuum deprecan—)

SUM PROVIDED   £200

AND THERE REMAINS THE SUM   £2,389. 2. 5 to be distributed according
to the form of the will

Thomas P ....   by us G. Chambye Auditors
                                J. Notte

From the abovewritten, Thomas Jermyn, one of the executors of the aforesaid Thomas Sprynge, promised in the presence of Master John Cockes, Chancellor to the lord archbishop of Canterbury, to distribute the underwritten sums in the form following, namely:

First, to Margaret who is to be married (maritand') to John Clopton, son and heir of William Clopton .... 500 marks

Also for Alice who is to be married to [2] Asshefeld .... 400 marks

Also for Anna who is to be married to [   ] Noone £100

Also for Elizabeth who is to be married to [   ] Henyngham £100

Also for Ursula who is to be married to [   ] Cokett .... 400 marks

Also for Maria who is to be married to [   ] Crane... 400 marks

Also for Barbara who is to be married to [   ] Scyntiorge £120

Also for their marriages to Thomas, Ambrose, Robert, Edmund and Anthony Jermyn, to each of them £50 ....£250

Also for the marriages of the four daughters of the said Thomas Jermyn, executor of the aforesaid Thomas Sprynge, to each of them £100, in total £400

Also towards the building of the bell-tower and making of the south aisle, part of the church of Lavenham (versus Reparac' Campanil' & performacionem Insule austral' partis ecclesie de laneham) £100

Also towards the repair of roads lying near Lavenham aforesaid................................£100

| SUM DISTRIBUTED | £2,303. 6. 8 |
| REMAINING | £85. 15. 9 |

[1] This phrase, "raised from the holy font", refers to the duties of godparents.

[2] In this and the following entries, no Christian names are given for the proposed husbands. Perhaps the planning of an alliance between families preceded the choice of actual individuals.

The atmosphere and texture of Lavenham are very different today from what they were before the Second World War. As can be seen in this view of Church Street, the accent is now on extensive restoration, exposure of timbers and a general smartness—the outward signs of profound economic and social change.

Bequests to Lavenham Church (1374-1540)

Name	Occupation (where known) Date and will reference	Details of gifts
Roger Madekot	[ ] 3/4/1374 Norwich 39 Heydon	To the fabric £6. 13. 4. For a mass book 40s.
Alan Waleys	Chaplain, 1385 Norwich 59 Harsyk	A psalter and a manual.
John Pelham	Rector, 11/11/1386 Norwich 74 Harsyk	To 13 the fabric 20s. A complete vestment for the priest at the altar of St Thomas the Martyr. Two surplices.
Matilda Faunt	[ ] c. 1392 SRO(B) 64 Osberne	To the reparation of the ornaments 6s. 8d.
Robert Frengge	Chaplain, 12/7/1403 Norwich 297 Harsyk	To the fabric 12d.
John Carpenter	Clothier, 2/10/1416 Norwich 18 Hyrnyng	To the emendation of the north part of the church 40s.
Robert Skarlet	Clothier, 5/11/1416 Norwich 12 Hyrnyng	A vestment for £10 and an antiphoner for 40s.
John Laggard	[ ] 10/6/1439 SRO(B) 14 Baldwyne	To the emendation of the church 20s.
John Place	Clothier, 10/3/1440 SRO(B) 24 Baldwyne	To the emendation of the church 40s.
Thomas Spring (I)	Clothier, 16/6/1440 SRO(B) 19 Baldwyne	To the fabric of the church 100s.
John Swayne	Tanner, 24/4/1441 SRO(B) 30 Baldwyne	To the emendation of the church 6s. 8d.
Agnes Helys	Widow, 10/8/1441 SRO(B) 31a Baldwyne	A low silver bowl to be made into 2 silver cruets to serve the high altar.
John Mey	[ ] 4/12/1443 SRO(B) 50 Baldwyne	To the emendation of the church 40d.
John Sadd	Rector, 25/8/1444 Norwich 50 Wylbey	To the fabric of the church 6s. 8d. A missal, a portable breviary and a silver basin.
William Bryan	Chaplain, 3/9/1445 Norwich 35 Wylbey	To the emendation of the church and the bell tower 13s. 4d. To the emendation of the ornaments 26s. 8d.

Name	Occupation (where known) Date and will reference	Details of gifts
Robert Taylonne	[ ] 17/5/1446 SRO(B) 91 Baldwyne	To the reparation of the church 20s.
John Pulkoo	[ ] 27/8/1447 SRO(B) 75 Baldwyne	To the fabric of the church 6s. 8d.
Thomas Rokell	[ ] 4/10/1447 SRO(B) 81 Baldwyne	For a font cover 8 marks.
John Persown	[ ] 29/7/1449 SRO (Ipswich) vol. 1, 77	To the emendation and reparation of the new works of Lavenham called the North Aisle £40.
John Sawyer	Clothier, 3/11/1449 SRO(B) 104 Baldwyne	To the fabric of the church 40s.
John Bownde	Weaver, 3/7/1452 SRO(B) 111 Baldwyne	For two cruets to serve in the church at the altar of St Katherine 40s.
John Archer	[ ] 3/10/1452 SRO(B) 139 Baldwyne	To the reparation of the church 6s. 8d.
Robert Joly	Butcher, 29/10/1456 Norwich 30 Neve	To the emendation of Lavenham church 40s.
Ralph Prior	[ ] 10/11/1456 Norwich 70 Neve	To the reparation of Lavenham church 26s. 8d.
Christiana Sturmyn	[ ] 6/3/1458 SRO(B) 211 Baldwyne	For a gold cloth for the high altar 10 marks.
Thomas Wyllymott	Clothier, 20/5/1459 SRO(B) 304 Baldwyne	To the reparation of Lavenham church 100s.
Agnes Mey	[ ] 20/1/1462 SRO(B) 345 Baldwyne	To the making or upkeep of the church 3s. 4d.
Andrew Grygges	[ ] 4/5/1462 SRO(B) 310 Baldwyne	To the reparation of Lavenham church 10 marks.
Margaret Beere	[ ] 28/8/1464 SRO(B) 381 Baldwyne	To the candlebeam in honour of the body of Christ 16s.
John Baker	Citizen and stockfishmonger of London, 17/10/1465 PCC 10 Godyn f.79	To the fabric of Lavenham church £20.
Thomas Skoyll	[ ] 6/2/1446? (proved 1466) Norwich 119 Cobbold	To the reparation of the church 40d.
Thomas Swan	Chaplain, 1/7/1467 Norwich 110 Betyns	To the reparation of the church 20s. To the altar of St Katherine the virgin a new gilt chalice, a new vestment of red colour and another of green to serve there in St Katherine's honour.

Name	Occupation (where known) Date and will reference	Details of gifts
William Schedde	[ ] 7/6/1469 SRO(B) 412 Baldwyne	For buying land for finding five lights to burn before the great image of the crucifix for ever £10 or more. To the reparation of the church 20s.
John Fermer	Aulnage collector, 23/9/1469 SRO(B) 81 Hervye	To the church a cloak of silk for £20.
John Sweyn	Tanner, 15/1/1470 SRO(B) 478 Baldwyne	To the reparation of the church 13s. 4d.
Joan Peck	[ ] 7/10/1473 SRO(B) 9 Hervye	To the reparation of the church 6s. 8d. Wax for a light for seven years before the image of the Blessed Mary on the north side of the church and for four years before image of St Christopher.
Richard Hadenham	Clothier, 6/4/1475 SRO(B) 142 Hervye	To the reparation of the church 20s.
Roger Crytott	Clothier, 7/4/1476 SRO(B) 52 Hervye	To the reparation of the church £10 (also reference to the image of St James the Apostle on the north side).
Margaret Tenwynter	Widow, 20/4/1476 SRO(B) 99 Hervye	To the reparation of the church 3s. 4d. To the altar of St Mary the Virgin a silver cloth.
Robert Grome	Clothier, 6/6/1476 SRO(B) 59 Hervye	To the reparation of the church—five long cloths.
Alice Woode	[ ] 8/8/1476 SRO(B) 68 Hervye	To the reparation of the church 5 marks.
Simon Joly	Butcher, 1/4/1477 SRO(B) 88 Hervye	To the reparation of the church 10s.
Joan Stoke	Widow, 15/5/1478 SRO(B) 161 Hervye	To the painting of the image of St Peter 40s. To the reparation of the church £5.
Robert Hervey	Priest, 10/6/1479 Norwich 238 Gelour	To the reparation of the organs 20s. To the reparation of the church 20s. To the church my book called The Golden Legend.[1]
Thomas Elot	Chaplain, 20/2/1485 Norwich 269 A. Caston	To the reparation of the church 40d.
Thomas Spring (II)	Clothier, 29/3/1486 PCC 25 Logge	To the building of the bell tower or the steeple of Lavenham Church 300 marks. To be buried in the vestry.[2]
William Seger	[ ] 5/1/1487 SRO(B) 431 Hervye	To the reparation of the church where necessary 20s.

[1] 'The Golden Legend' or Legenda Aurea was a manual consisting mainly of lives of the saints.
[2] The brass of Thomas Spring II can still be seen in the vestry.

Name	Occupation (where known) Date and will reference	Details of gifts
Aleyn Sexten	Clothier, 26/12/1487 PCC 7 Milles	To the making of the steeple of Lavenham £40.
William Joly	Butcher, – 1488 SRO(B) 399 Hervye	To the church of Lavenham 20s.
Roger Braunche	Clothier, 9/3/1489 PCC 24 Milles	To the making of the steeple £20. For a mass book to the Trinity altar 10 marks. Buried before the image of the Blessed Trinity.
Nicholas Gosselyn	Clothier, 24/6/1491 PCC 46 Milles	To the reparation and garnishing of the images of Our Lady, St John, St Christopher and St Anthony 13s. 4d.
John Dyx	[ ] 12/10/1492 SRO(B) 27 Boner	To the church of Lavenham 20s.
John Fuller	Mercer, 14/12/1492 PCC 21 Dogget	To the reparation of the church £10.
Ralf Hancocke	Clothier, – 1493 PCC 28 Dogget	To the reparation of the church £5.
Robert Reynold	Priest, 6/8/1493 Norwich 142 Typpes	To Lavenham church my 'prykton' book and my little processionary full necessary to this church.[3]
James Spring	Clothier, 29/8/1493 PCC 4 Vox	To the making of the steeple £40. If the wife is not with child a further £33. 6. 8d. for Lavenham steeple. To be buried in the vestry.
Thomas Sturmyn	Clothier, 4/10/1493 PCC 3 Vox	To the reparation of the church 10 marks.
William Sturmyn	Clothier, 22/10/1493 PCC 4 Vox	To the reparation of the church £20.
Robert Parle	[ ] 12/11/1493 SRO(B) 444 Hervye	To the reparation of the church 20s.
Rose Grome	Widow, 16/5/1494 SRO(B) 91 Boner	To the making of an arch in the church £20.
John Baxster	[ ] 4/11/1494 SRO(B) 24 Boner	To the making of the steeple 4 marks. To Our Lady's light in the chapel a red bullock.
Thomas Braunche	Clothmaker, 13/3/1498 PCC 32 Horne	To the new making and reparation of the church £10.
William Jacob	Clothier, 26/9/1500 Norwich 115 Cage	To the church of Lavenham £20.
Elizabeth Braunche	Widow, 10/1/1501 PCC 11 Blamyr	To the reparation of the church 100 marks.

[3] 'Prykton' refers to musical notation which was "pricked" on the page rather than written.

Name	Occupation (where known) Date and will reference	Details of gifts
Simon Braunche	Batchelor/Clothier, 4/7/1502 SRO(B) 138 Boner	To the new building of the church 20s.
Joan Sexton	Widow, 9/8/1502 PCC 20 Blamyr	To the new building of the church £10.
John Newton	Clothmaker, 14/10/1502 PCC 20 Blamyr	To the reparation of the church 26s. 8d.
Elizabeth Wyllymott	Widow, 27/7/1504 PCC 19 Holgrave	For painting the image of St Peter at the high altar 40s.—20s. more if necessary. For making a window in the south aisle with two images of St Peter and St Paul £5.
John Rysby	Clothier, 9/8/1504 PCC 20 Holgrave	To the edifying of Lavenham church £200 by the advice of the Earl of Oxford to discharge conscience.
Richard Prykke	[ ] 7/9/1504 SRO(B) 156 Boner	To the building of the church 20s.
Edmund Bownde	Clothier, 20/12/1504 PCC 25 Holgrave	To the making and reparation of the church 40s. Robert, his son, to have a window glazed on the south side in remembrance of him.
Robert Smyth	Priest, 7/1/1505 Norwich 336 Ryxe	To the building of the church 20s.
Agnes Braunche	Widow, 18/2/1506 PCC 23 Adeane	To the reparation of the church 40s. To be buried in the 'new aisle'.
William Rysby	Clothier, 23/8/1506 PCC 12 Adeane	To the reparation of the church £10.
John Spyltymber	Cordwainer, 26/4/1507 Norwich, 1 Spyltymber	His daughter Alice from her legacy to pay to the new aisle door 40s.
Christopher Bonefaunt	[ ] 14/6/1507 PCC 25 Adeane	For a silver and gilt crown for the image of Our Lady 'the which is worshipped with divers oblations' 5 nobles.[4]
Roger Reignold	Husbandman, 27/8/1510 PCC 33 Bennett	His wife to have done the painting of Our Lady of Pity to value of 20s.
13th Earl of Oxford	Lord of capital manor, 10/5/1513 PCC 11 Fettiplace	Towards the making of the aisles of Lavenham church £20, besides the £20 already given to the same.
Robert Sexten the Elder	Clothier, 25/2/1517 PCC 6 Ayloffe	To the building of the steeple if they will set thereupon within 2 years £40.
John Shedd	Clothmaker, 12/11/1517 PCC 16 Maynwaryng	To the reparation of the church 20s.

[4] A noble was worth 6s 8d, or half a mark.

Name	Occupation (where known) Date and will reference	Details of gifts
Thomas Stansby	Clothmaker, 19/4/1518 PCC 13 Ayloffe	For an altar cloth of gold £10. For a pair of organs to keep Our Lady's mass £8. For a pair of candlesticks of latten for the high altar 40s. For 2 copes for the Rector £10. To be buried in the chapel of the Holy Trinity.
William Hogge	Carrier, 21/10/1518 SRO(B) 105 Fuller	To the glazing of the steeple 20s.
Robert Rysby	Clothier, 20/1/1520 PCC 4 Maynwaryng	To the building of the steeple £3.
Miles Wytton	Clothmaker, 23/1/1520 PCC 6 Maynwaryng	To the making of the steeple 20s. To the canopy that should be made at the high altar if within 2 years 20s.
John Pondyr	Clothmaker, 5/6/1520 PCC 30 Ayloffe	To the building of the steeple 4 marks.
Agnes Sexten	Widow of clothier, 20/7/1520 PCC 31 Ayloffe	To the building of the steeple £40. For a candlebeam £100. For a 'foote' before St Anne 20s.
Simon Causton	Clothmaker, 18/2/1521 PCC 7 Maynwaryng	To the reparation of the steeple £18. To the gilding of the tabernacle of Our Lady, in the chapel on the south side of the church £8. To the building of the steeple £40, which he was judged to pay for discharging his conscience.
Thomas Barbour	Clothier, 22/1/1523 PCC 17 Bodfelde	To be buried in the chapel of Our Lady of Five Joys.
Simon Clogg	Clothmaker, 10/4/1523 PCC 9 Bodfelde	To the building of the steeple £20.
Thomas Spring (III)	Clothier, 13/6/1523 PCC 11 Bodfelde	To the finishing of the steeple of Lavenham £200.[5] To be buried in Lavenham church before the altar of St Katherine where I will be made a tomb with a parclose thereabout.
John Fermer	[ ] 3/12/1523 PCC 16 Bodfelde	To the making of a new cross in the churchyard £20.
Roger Trype	Clothier, 2/12/1526 PCC 1 Thrower	To the gilding of the tabernacle of St Peter £6. 13. 4d.
Agnes Rysby	Widow, 18/8/1528 SRO(B) 219 Johnson	To gilding the tabernacle of St Peter 40s.

[5] His executors spent a further £847 on the church and its furnishings. See p. 14 and Appendix 1.

Name	Occupation (where known) Date and will reference	Details of gifts
Joan Fermore	Widow, 5/11/1529 SRO(B) 13 Longe	To Lavenham church a cross of £26. 13. 4d. to be made within 4 years.
Edmund Smythe	[ ] 19/5/1531 SRO(B) 77 Longe	To the gilding of the tabernacle of St Peter 7s.
Alice Spring	Widow, 13/4/1538 PCC 21 Dyngeley	For the reparation of the church £6. 13. 4d.
John Hunt	Clothier, 20/1/1539 PCC 6 Alenger	To the honour of God to the reparation of the church of Lavenham 2 wetcloths the one to be a blue and the other a vess.
Robert Grome	Clothier, 28/8/1540 PCC 16 Alenger	To the reparation of the church £20.

The Spring parclose in the north aisle of Lavenham Church, carved about 1525. Notice the intricate detail of this superb carving; for example, the two tiny figures holding the coat of arms of Thomas Spring III.

Bequests to Lavenham Gilds (1416–1540)

Name	Occupation (where known) Date and will reference	Details of gifts
John Carpenter	Clothier, 2/10/1416 Norwich 18 Hyrnyng	To the fraternal Gild of the Holy Trinity in Lavenham 40s.
Geoffrey Godryche	Chaplain, 6/7/1423 Norwich 122 Hyrnyng	To the brethren of the Gild of St Peter and St Paul 6s. 8d.
Robert Taylonne	[ ] 17/5/1446 SRO(B) 91 Baldwyne	To the Gild of St Peter and St Paul for the stipend of a chaplain of the same 6s. 8d.
Thomas Wyllymot	Clothier, 20/5/1459 SRO(B) 304 Baldwyne	To the Gild of St Peter to support the priest 100s.
William Schedde	[ ] 7/6/1469 SRO(B) 412 Baldwyne	To the fraternity of the Gild of the Holy Trinity of Lavenham to buy lands, tenements or rents for a priest to celebrate divine service for ever in the church for the souls of the brothers and sisters of the fraternity £20. The Alderman of the Gild of the Holy Trinity of Lavenham to have the gift and disposition of six houses for the poor of Lavenham time without end.
John Harry	Clothier, 28/3/1473 SRO(B) 536 Baldwyne	To the Gild of the Holy Trinity to buy 'as much livelihood as will provide a chaplain to celebrate divine service in Lavenham church for the souls of the same fraternity . . .' 10 marks.
Roger Crytott	Clothier, 7/4/1476 SRO(B) 52 Hervye	To be invested for the Gild of the Holy Trinity to provide a chaplain (as above) £20. Refers to the brothers and sisters of the Gild.
Robert Parsons	[ ] 15/10/1477 SRO(B) 178 Hervye	To the Gild of Corpus Christi in Lavenham 6s. 8d.
Thomas Elot	Chaplain, 20/2/1485 Norwich 269 A. Caston	To the Gild or fraternity of the Holy Trinity 20s.
William Joly	Butcher, —1488 SRO(B) 399 Hervye	Mentions the *stall* of St Peter's Gild in the Market Place.
John Dyx	[ ] 12/10/1492 SRO(B) 27 Boner	To the chaplain of the Gild of St Peter to celebrate a trental 10s.[1] To the Gild of St Peter for torches at obsequies 6s. 8d.

[1] A trental is thirty masses said for the soul of a dead person.

Name	Occupation (where known) Date and will reference	Details of gifts
Ralf Hancocke	Clothier, —1493 PCC 28 Dogett	To the Gild of SS Peter & Paul 10s. To the same for a trental 10s.
Robert Parle	[ ] 12/11/1493 SRO(B) 444 Hervye	To the Gild of SS Peter & Paul 3s. 4d.
John Rysby	Clothier, 16/5/1493 PCC 25 Dogett	To the Gild of SS Peter & Paul desiring to become a brother and to be partaker of their prayers, on this condition 6s. 8d.
William Sturmyn	Clothier, 22/10/1493 PCC 4 Vox	To the Gild of St Peter £3. 6. 8d.
John Baxster	[ ] 4/11/1494 SRO(B) 24 Boner	To the Trinity Gild a brass pot of 7 gallons.
William Jacob	Clothier, 26/9/1500 Norwich 115 Cage	For a banner cloth for Our Lady's Gild 40s.
Joan Rosell	[ ] 15/2/1503 SRO(B) 62 Fuller	To the Gild of St Peter and St Paul 6 pewter platters. To Sir Geoffrey, priest of the Gild, for a trental 10s.
Richard Prykke	[ ] 7/9/1504 SRO(B) 156 Boner	To the Gild of the Assumption of Our Lady 6s. 8d.
Edmund Bownde	Clothier, 20/12/1504 PCC 25 Holgrave	To the Gild of St Peter & St Paul a great mazer, 12 pieces of pewter and a table cloth.
Roger Reignold	Husbandman, 27/8/1510 PCC 33 Bennett	To the Gild of St Peter 20s.
Miles Wytton	Clothmaker, 23/1/1520 PCC 6 Maynwaryng	To the Gild of Corpus Christi a tenement in the High Street.
Simon Clogg	Clothmaker, 10/4/1523 PCC 9 Bodfelde	To Our Lady's Gild for its maintenance 40s.
John Byrde the Elder	Clothmaker, 3/6/1524 PCC 25 Bodfelde	To the Gild of Our Lady 10s.
Roger Trype	Clothier, 2/12/1526 PCC 1 Thrower	To the Gild of St Peter to the reparation of the hall and the barn of the same Gild £4.
Joan Bretunne	[ ] 2/12/1527 SRO(B) 227 Brydon	To the Gild of St Peter 2s. 8d. To the Gild of St Christopher 2s. 8d.[2]
Agnes Rysby	Widow, 18/8/1528 SRO(B) 219 Johnson	To the Gild of St Peter my silver salt.
Roger Bretton	[ ] 5/2/1528 SRO(B) 59 Longe	To St Peter's Gild 6s. 8d. To St Christopher's Gild 3s. 4d.[2]

[2] St Christopher's Gild was probably in another, unknown, parish.

Name	Occupation (where known) Date and will reference	Details of gifts
John Lymmour	Fuller and Clothmaker, 4/2/1528 PCC 2 Jankyn	To the Gild of Our Lady 40s.
Joan Smythe	Widow, 5/4/1540 SRO(B) 112 Poope	To St Peter's Gild 6s. 8d.

The Corpus Christi Gildhall has an original oriel window facing Lady Street, and the cornerpost bears a human figure said to represent John de Vere, 15th Earl of Oxford.

APPENDIX 4

Bequests to Lavenham Highways (1386-1544)

Name	Occupation (where known) Date and will reference	Details of gifts
John Pelham	Rector, 11/11/1386 Norwich 74 Harsyk	For the road to Sudbury next to Lavenham rectory 20s.
Robert Skarlet	Clothier, 5/11/1416 Norwich 12 Hyrnyng	To the emendation of the roads about Lavenham where they are most defective £10.
Thomas Hervey	Chaplain, 14/1/1417 Norwich 47 Hyrnyng	To the emendation of a road in a bad state up to Hamelyngs next to Sarlro green 6s. 8d.
Thomas Spring I	Clothier, 16/6/1440 SRO(B) 19 Baldwyne	To the reparation of the highway from Lavenham to Bury St Edmunds 9 marks.
Katherine Wasshman	[ ] 16/4/1441 SRO(B) 30 Baldwyne	To the emendation of a road to Sarbys Green 40d.
William Curby	[ ] 12/10/1453 SRO(B) 159 Baldwyne	To the emendation of the highway between Lavenham and Sudbury 20s.
Ralph Prior	[ ] 10/11/1456 Norwich 70 Neve	To the emendation of the highway from the churchyard gate to 'le parsones cros' 40s. and from the same cross to the croft called Hamelyns 40s.
Thomas Willymot	Clothier, 20/5/1459 SRO(B) 304 Baldwyne	To the reparation of the highway before my gate 20s.
Agnes Mey	[ ] 20/1/1462 SRO(B) 345 Baldwyne	To the reparation of the highway next to the churchyard 20s.
John Newman	Clothier, 21/3/1463 SRO (B) 335 Baldwyne	To the emendation of the high roads around the town of Lavenham £40.
William Schedde	[ ] 7/6/1469 SRO(B) 412 Baldwyne	To the emendation of the highway between Boxford and Lavenham 4 marks.
John Fermer	Aulnage Collector, 23/9/1469 SRO(B) 81 Hervye	I wish that the highway opposite my house in Lavenham be completely made up with sand beginning at my renter[1] and proceeding to the north end of the street (no sum mentioned).
John Harry	Clothier, 28/3/1473 SRO(B) 536 Baldwyne	To the emendation of the highway to Eleigh Combust 10 marks.
Roger Crytott	Clothier, 7/4/1476 SRO(B) 536 Baldwyne	To the reparation of the highways in Lavenham £20.

[1] A "renter" in this sense is not a person but a property rented out.

Name	Occupation (where known) Date and will reference	Details of gifts
Richard Hadenham	Clothier, 6/4/1475 SRO(B) 142 Hervye	To the reparation of the highway in the street called Master John Street 10s.
Harry Pulcoo	Weaver, 20/2/1476 SRO(B) 102 Hervye	The bridge at my door to be sufficiently made for all manner of people to pass over on foot at my proper cost.
Simon Joly	Butcher, 1/4/1477 SRO(B) 88 Hervye	To amending of the highway at Mortymer Hill Lavenham 20s.
Thomas Spring II	Clothier, 29/3/1486 PCC 25 Logge	To the reparation of the broken roads about Lavenham 200 marks.
William Seger	[ ] 5/1/1487 SRO(B) 431 Hervye	To the emendation of the road between Lavenham and Bury 20s.
Thomas Sturmyn	Clothier, 4/10/1493 PCC 3 Vox	To the amending of the foul way between Lavenham and Melford 5 marks.
William Sturmyn	Clothier, 22/10/1493 PCC 4 Vox	To the highways about the town of Lavenham £10.
William Jacob	Clothier, 26/9/1500 Norwich 115 Cage	To the mending of highways about Lavenham 100 marks, that is to say 40 marks between Sudbury and Lavenham and 20 marks between Lavenham and Cock-field and 20 marks between Lavenham and Brent Eleigh and 20 marks between Laven-ham and Bridge Street.
Thomas Rysby	Clothier, 18/12/1500 PCC 14 Blamyr	To repair the way from Lavenham to Melford £20.
John Rysby	Clothier, 9/8/1504 PCC 20 Holgrave	To the highways 100 marks of his father's goods as it should please the Earl of Oxford, supervisor of his father's will.
Christopher Bonefaunt	[ ] 14/6/1507 PCC 25 Adeane	To amending the highways next to the town of Lavenham 30s.
Thomas Parker	Clothman, 4/5/1516 PCC 17 Holder	To the reparation of the highway before my door and to the market 13s. 4d.
Simon Clogg	Clothmaker, 12/11/1517 PCC 9 Bodefelde	To the amending of the highway from the cross up towards the church of Lavenham £5.
William Hogge	Carrier, 21/10/1518 SRO(B) 105 Fuller	To amend the highway between Coggys and Huntys Grene 46s. 8d.
Agnes Sexten	Widow and clothier, 20/2/1520 PCC 31 Ayloffe	For the reparation of the highways £40.
John Fermer	[ ] 3/12/1523 PCC 16 Bodefelde	To the reparation of the highway between Colls Croft and the tenter yard towards St Edmundsbury 40s.

Name	Occupation (where known) Date and will reference	Details of gifts
Thomas Spring III	Clothier, 13/6/1523 PCC 11 Bodfelde	To the reparation of the highways about the town of Lavenham 100 marks.[2]
John Lymmour	Fuller and clothmaker, 4/2/1528 PCC 2 Jankyn	For mending the highway towards Bury £10.
Alice Spring	Widow, 13/4/1538 PCC 21 Dyngeley	To amending the highways between Lavenham and Groton £40.
John Hunt	Clothier, 20/1/1539 PCC 6 Alenger	To the highway between Lavenham and Melford £15.
John Barker	Clothmaker, 31/10/1544 PCC 17 Pynnyng	To repairing the highways between the town of Bildeston and Ipswich £20.

His executors spent a further £166 13s 4d on the repair of roads. See Appendix 1.

Around Lavenham narrow roads, traditionally ditched and hedged, wind across heavy clay country. Before modern surfaces were introduced they were always difficult to maintain and drain.

Two Lavenham Inventories

A. Inventory of John Tarver, Worsted Weaver of Lavenham, 1696
SRO(B): IC 500/3/25 (91)
(*Note:* to aid the reader, pound weight is distinguished from pound money. Otherwise, the transcript follows the original exactly. A glossary of terms can be found on pp. 125-127).

A True Inventory of all and singular the Goods & Chattells Rights Creditts and Personall Estate of John Tarver late of Lavenham in the County of Suffolk Worsted weaver deceased made taken & valued by us whose names are hereunto subscribed the 22th day of May Anno Domini 1696.

	£	s	d
In his Warehouse Woollchambers and working shopps			
Loose silk and silk upon Bobbins valued all at six pounds	6	0	0
24 peses of Callamanco	67	4	0
6 peses of Ancerins	18	0	0
7 half peses of Tamarins	9	9	0
2 hole peses of Tamarins	4	6	0
4 short peses of Tames stripes	5	0	0
5 Sholons	9	15	0
22 yards Tamerin	1	0	0
2 yards 2/2 [sic] of Cloth & 3 yards of Cloth & 12 yards of dimety	1	12	0
A Remnant of Cors stuf	0	5	0
in Ruf Wooll 5 scoer & 8 lb	5	17	0
Clothing wooll 87 lb £2 3s. & Lokes 25 lb: 5s.	2	8	0
Scored Niles 7 scoer & 5 lb	3	12	6
Grasey Niles 36 lb	0	12	0
pouls 80 lb	0	16	8
7 scoer and 2 lb of Long Reld Yarne spun to A Leaven pound fouer shilens & ninpence	22	9	6
2 grose of grasey yarne £1 10s. 0d. & 10 dusen of blew yarne and yarne upon bobens 18s. 7d.	2	8	7
A parcel of smoll Cord with A peese of harp string	0	0	9
Fine scored Topes 16 scoer & 2 lb	26	16	4
Say Topes 18 lb at £1 2s. 6d. Cors topes 10 lb at 10s. & grasey topes 2 scoer & 14 lb at £3 10s. 6d.	5	3	0
9 Lomes with the taklen blongen to them	8	4	0
one bame scales & waits belongin to them	0	11	0
one shiftenen bord & 2 tresels to it	0	2	6
on Twistin Mill & A Warpen Mill & treues with the bobens & All belongen to to [sic] the Mills	3	10	0
A payer of Ringes & 2 ould scouren tubes	0	6	0
on fram on Pres on fram to mak up peses with the Irons to them & yarn poles	0	11	6
wooll sceps A bame with bras scals	0	10	6
A smol bam at spiners with sum waits	0	3	0
A Litel silk whel & 2 payer of Rises with a Roul	0	5	0

	£	s	d
2 smole ould Clouths with A Cord & A Load of Coole	3	2	0
A hardel A payer of old Comes & other smol trifels	0	4	0
[ ] 0 4 4 tow or thre old Vates	[		]

In the Kitchen

	£	s	d
Two oval Tables with wings	1	0	0
fouer Lether Chayers six borded Chaiers thre Rush botumd Chaiers one high Childs Chaier one Childs Wicker Chaier and A wooden stoole A skrien of five Laves Clothed with Lincie-Woolice A wicker Cradle A spice box & salt box A Glas Case & tow pickturs	2	5	10
one pres dresser & tow shelves an A poot bord	0	16	0
one musket A fouling pes & tow ould pistils A hanger and A bagonet	1	10	0
one Clock & the Case 50s. one Jack A Chane & tow spitts 12s.	3	2	0
32 peses of peuter waid 77 lb at 8d. lb	2	11	4
6 pewter porengers sum of them smole	0	2	0
4 dos. of pewter plates £2 and 10 ould smoler plats 5s.	2	5	0
one warming pann 4s. & 6 bras Candel sticks & 2 bras Chafing dishes A bras snuff pan and snufers	0	14	0
A Candel box A tine pott 2 hand Candelsticks A smal grid-iron A choping knife & 4 Arthen plates A smal iron Candel stick A droper & slice	0	5	0
4 bibles & A feue other smal bookes	0	12	0
one payer of Cob Irons firpan & tongues tow tramels 2 flower pots 2 window curtanes & 2 Rods and A payer of bellows	0	13	4
one smoothing Iron 3 heters & A Reast & drinken potts & glases A payr of wood Racks & part of A Suger Loafe	0	6	0
A Larg Iron porege pott with A brass Lid to it	0	10	0

In the Buteries

	£	s	d
7 beere vesels 35s. 4 Ale stooles 2 poudring tubes & 2 sives A deal dreser with 3 drauers A smole morter & pestill	2	15	2
one dusen of pattie pans A basting Ladel A Cliver A fork A tin Cover A culendur A tunel A drudging box A dripping pan A Grat A roulingpin A tinder box one dusen of trenchers A pudding dish tow grate goches & some other Earthinware A woodin boule dish	0	14	2
one dusen & half of knives A 11 forks & 2 or 3 shelves	0	6	0
A kneading trough A frying pan A tind boiler A sawce pan A hanging skillet & 3 other skilets A skummer A Litele kettel A chafingdish & a gridiron	1	13	0
2 Lanthorns A wooden forme & stoole A feue ould woodden dishes & some other trifels A few more shelves	0	4	0
4 dus & 4 glase bottels 8s. tow Kitels waid 27 lb	1	15	8

In the bruhous

	£	s	d
one large mishing tubb & on smoler one koule & seven kelers Clense A meshing staf A jett an Eal stol A washing keler and 2 pailes	2	2	0

In the Parlour

	£	s	d
one ovel Tabel with winges one Litel square Tabel Eight Leather Chayers one Couch with the Appurtenances	2	18	0
one paire of Cobirons firpan and tongues all with brases and one payer of bellows	0	9	0
one Curtain rod and 2 window curtains and thurteen pinted pictures	0	18	0

117

In the hall

one Long tabel & fouer buffet stooles one ould Cubard one ould box A strikeing bord tow ould rustey rapers one ould plank stoole A case of shelves nine pound of hopes and an ould hamper bridel & shakel an ould carpet and A deale horse   1   14   0

In the Parlour Chamber

	£	s	d
one posted bedsted with sad Culerd serge valans and Curtins	2	0	0
one fetherbed one father bolster and 2 father pillows waid 102 lb at 12d. per lb	5	2	0
one quilt and tow blankets	1	10	0
Six Cane Chayers and thre old surge Chaires	2	5	0
One Tabel and tow stands A dresing box A komb box & 4 smal boxes	1	10	0
one payre Crepers with bras heads	0	2	0
one Chest of drawers on Looken glass the hangings of the Roome A Curtan Rod and tow small window Curtins	3	18	0

In the hall Chamber

	£	s	d
one posted beadstad with red Chaney valens & Curtains	1	2	6
one father bed one father boulster & tow father pillows waid 71 lb at 8d. per lb & thre blankets one old quilt	3	7	4
one Chest of drawers & one table one trunke & tow old boxes	1	6	6
one ould serge Chayer fouer Rush bottumd Chayers A Cribe A Cushen tow Litel window Curtains & A Curtain Rod & tow or thre trifels	0	12	4

In the gate house Chamber

	£	s	d
one Litel Canopy bedsted with A back & tow Curtins of printed Calico & tow blankets & A counter penne	1	1	0
Thre old Chayers A Littel form A windo Curtain and Rod	0	4	0
one father bed on father boulster & 3 father pillowes waid 49 lb	1	16	9

one the staire head

one Larg trunk one Chast & one box   0   16   0

In the Mens Loging Rome

	£	s	d
one posted beadstad with A Lincie Woolcie Tester and Curtins	0	10	0
one old fatherbed one father bolster and tow pillows waid 66 lb at 6d. per lb	1	13	0
one sad Culerd Rugg two ould blankets & A window Curtin	0	10	6
Copper Irons & door waid 1 cwt 3 qr 4 lb at 2d. lb	1	13	4

In A Closet

	£	s	d
one silver Tankerd one silver porenger Eight spoons Thre salts some broken buttens & other Littel things & Clipt money waid 46 ounses A half not all starling silver	11	12	0
one 20s. peice of old broad gold & 2 gold Ringgs	2	2	0
Tow tipt woodden potts A silver hafted knife and fork	0	4	0
14 Coffe Cupes 5 other Urthin dishes	0	6	0

The Linen

	£	s	d
one damask Board Cloth and one dusen of damask napkins	2	5	0
one diaper Board Cloth & 12 napkins	1	18	0
one dosen of Corser diaper napkins & 2 board cloths	0	13	0
one Tabel Cloth & six napkins nine napkins & board Cloth	0	9	6
one paier of holand shets & 2 pillow biers	2	5	0
one paire of holland sheetes & three pillow biers	0	16	6

	£	s	d
one larg then holland sheet A payer shets A payr of pillowbiers	0	18	0
one paier small sheets & 2 pillowbiers	0	8	0
tow paier of shets & three pillowbiers	1	3	0
one paier of shets & 2 pillowbiers 2 smol old table cloths	0	10	0
one payer of hempen sheets & 2 old pillowbiers	0	11	0
tow paier of hempen sheets & eight old sheet A half sheet	1	13	0
Eight old touels & A smoothing Cloth A remnant of new Cloth	0	6	0
six loose Irish sticht Covers for Cushens	0	15	0
A Childs basket & pin Cushion & A parcel of Childbed Linnen	7	5	6
his wearing Apparell of All Sorts	10	0	0
7 ould napkens	0	1	4
debts good and bad	28	16	0
[ ] 17–10			
A watch	3	0	0

Totall this Inventory Errors in casting up if any onely excepted
Is   £347. 4s. 11d.

	347	4	11
	35	10	0
	382	14	11

An addition to 5 July   John Pinchbeck ⎤
                          William Bexwell ⎟ Apprisors
                          Nicholas Garnon ⎦

Item A Bed and furniture vallued with a
Horse Bridle & saddle   at   £32   0. 0d.
A sword   2   0. 0d.
Two badd Debts due
John Beedon & Jon Lamb   1 10. 0d.
                                       ―――――――――――
                                       35 10. 0d.

        mk. of
Geo   ×   King

Elizabeth Tarver
        [signed]

[Proved 10 June 1696]

B. Inventory of John Pinchbecke, Woollen Draper of Lavenham, 1704

SRO(B): IC500/3/32(20) A glossary of terms can be found on pp. 125–127.

An Inventory of the goods and Chattells of John Pinchbecke late of Lavenham in the county of Suffolk, woollen draper valued and apprised the 12th day of Aprill Anno Domini 1704 by Henry Boughton and John Culpick.

	£	s	d
3 pieces of white Shalloones at 38s. per peice	5	14	0
30½ yds. of druggett at 2s. 3d. per yard	3	18	7½[sic]
5 peices of Norwich stuffs all	5	8	0
2 remnants of Burying Crape	3	11	0
a parcell of Stuffs in 10 severall remnants	1	17	0
a parcell of Stuffs in 6 severall remnants	1	5	6
13½ yards of watered Cheny, black at 16d. yard	0	18	0
5¼ yds. of black Barratine 13 yds. mohair in 5 remnants	1	11	0
16 yds.⅜ of mohair in 4 remnants	1	19	0
19½ yds. of Tabbys and halfe silk stuffs in 19 remnants	3	7	0
37 yards of Stuffs in 11 severall remnants	2	10	9
14½ yds of Stuffs in 6 severall remnants	0	12	0
27 yds. of black and white Crape in 4 remnants	1	5	10
17 yds. of Norwich druggett at 11d. yard	0	15	7
25 yds. ½ of dammaske at in 3 remnants	1	7	8
15 yds of grey narrow Cloth at 3s. 4d. yard	2	10	0
14 yds. of narrow Cloth in 6 remnants	2	12	10
22¼ yds. of ffrieze at 3s. 9d. yard in 2 remnants	4	3	5
4¾ yds. of black Cloth serge in 2 remnants at 3s. 9d. yard	0	12	8 [sic]
15¾ yds. of Cloth serge at 2s. 9d. yard	2	3	3½
12 yds. of Cloth serge at 2s. 6d. yard	1	10	0
12 yds. of sagitta and serges in 5 severall remnants all	1	2	0
18½ yds. of Sad Coloured Cotton at 14d. yard all	1	1	0 [sic]
9½ yds of white flannell in 3 remnants at 20d. yard	0	15	10
10¼ yds of black broadcloth at 10s. yard	5	2	6
10 yds. of black broadcloth at 8s. yard	4	0	0
17 yds. of Broad Cloth in 4 remnants at 7s. 6d. yard	6	7	6
9 3/8 yds. of broadcloth in 8 remnants	2	18	9
27¼ yds. of Colchester bays at 20d. yard	2	5	5
29½ yds. of cotton at 14d. yard	1	14	5
1 piece & 6¼ yds. of black Cloth Rash all	4	13	6
9 yellow wastcoates at	1	5	6
10 small yellow wastcoates at		7	2
20¾ yds. of scarlett and black flannell at 2s. 6d. yard	2	11	10
23¾ yds. of toulon serges in 2 remnants at 2s. 6d. yard	2	19	4½
59½ yds. of perpetuanoes at 20d. yard in 4 remnants	4	19	2
9 yds. of ell wide serge at 29d. yard	1	4	9
9 yds. of druggett at 2s. 2d. yard	0	19	6
108 yds. ½ of dyed Shalloones in 9 remnants at 18d. yard	8	2	9
4 yds. of sad colourd serge at 2s. yard	0	8	0
14 yds. ½ of black serge at 2s. 4d. yard	1	13	10
5¾ yds. of Serge in 3 remnants	0	10	6
10½ sad coulour serge at 20d. yard	0	17	6
12¾ say at 18d. per yard	0	19	1½

	£	s	d
3¼ yds. of blew [ ] at	0	12	0
18 yds. of white houndscote say at 18d. [ ] yard	1	1	0 [sic]
2¾ yds. of druggett and 3 yds. of green bays in 2 remnants	0	5	9
14½ yds. of flowerd satten at 20d. yd.	1	4	2
22 yds. of damaske in 5 remnants	1	0	0
60½ yds. of Norwch. Stuffes in 6 remnants at	1	19	0
12¼ yds. of Shag in 3 remnants all	2	10	6
29½ yds. of Turkia Tamet at in 3 remnants	1	16	0
20¼ yds. of Turkia mohair in 3 remnants	1	8	3½
36¾ yds. of Tamet all	1	2	1½
21½ yds. of worsted Farrendine in several remnants all	1	0	0
28¾ yds. of Tamerine at 9d. yard	1	1	6
54 yds. ¼ of worsted Stuffs in 15 remnants	2	8	9
a Black Cloth Roll	1	0	0
3 yds. of white flannell	0	3	3
30 washed Skins at 9s. douzen	1	2	6
3 lbs. 9 oz. belladine silk at 23s. per lb	4	2	0
a Parcell of old braided galloones	0	18	0
4 peices of plaine silk galloone	1	0	0
2 douzen of thrid galloone	0	1	6
2 peices of Ghentings	1	10	0
1 end of dyed Fustian	1	8	0
99¼ yds. of colourd fustian in 8 remnants all	4	18	4½
29 yds. ¾ of white fustian in 9 remnants at	1	3	0
6½ ells of Holland in 4 remnants	0	16	9
4 small remnants of Holland	0	2	0
4¼ yds. of Canvas	0	5	0
1 piece of diaper	0	10	0
9¾ yds. of Holland diaper	0	14	6
2 remnants of Huckaback	0	5	6
35½ ells of Osnabrix at	1	7	10
27 ells of Flaxing Cloth at 6d. ¾ per ell	0	15	2
5 yds. ½ of Bores Laps	0	5	0
13 ells of Irish Cloth in 2 remnants	0	11	6
4 remnants of holland 5½ yds. of white Calleco	0	18	0
10 ells of Alkinore holland	1	0	0
5 remnants of Linnen Cloth	0	10	6
18½ ells of Garlick Holland all	1	9	5
3 remnants of Garlick holland	0	3	6
11 yds. of Scotch Cloth at 14d. yard	0	12	10
22 yds. ½ of painted Calleco all	1	15	3
remnants of Calleco and Muslin	0	12	2
5 yds. of Muslin all	0	13	4
15½ yds. of blew and white Linnen at 8d. yard	0	10	4
13 yds. blew calleco and a remnant all	0	17	9
19¼ yds. narrow blew linnen at 7d. yard	0	11	0 [sic]
8 remnants of blew Linnen	0	7	5
177¾ yards of Hemping Cloth in 11 remnants all	9	12	6
17 yds. Cheese Cloth in 3 remnants at 7d. yard	0	9	11
39½ yds. of died Linnen and buccoram in severall remnants	1	7	5
A Childs burying suit and loose peices of crape	0	3	0
Coloured blew and white handkerchiefes	0	3	0

	£	s	d
25 yds. Linnen Cloth at	0	13	10
Silver Braid and Remnants of silver Lace and silver galloone	1	9	4
Silk braid and Cord and 5 dousen of silk buttons	0	9	8
Fforrett Ribbons	0	18	0
worsted	0	15	6
11 silk handkerchiefs	0	19	6
Remnants of Muslin and girdles	0	4	6
A parcell broad Ribbons	2	10	0
12 yds. of Orris	0	8	0
2 remnants black fring and 2 peices worsted	0	8	0
8 pair of Childs hose and metall buttons	0	15	0
6 pair of black hose at	0	11	0
15 pair of hose at	2	5	6
14 pair of hose at	1	1	4
Laces pins tapes and fillittings	4	5	7
7 pair of bodys and 3 stomachers	1	6	0
Packthrid bodys and stiff bucceram	0	4	0
5 lb ½ whited thrid 3s. 4d. per lb	0	18	4
32 lb ½ of black, browne and Colourd thrid	2	19	5
3 lb of blew thrid	0	6	0

This high-quality Tudor house, incorporating a shop, occupies a prominent corner at the bottom of Lady Street. Notice how this has affected the angle of the joists holding up the jetty.

	£	s	d
6 lb and 1 ounce ½ of fine thrid of severall sorts all	1	16	2
Silk Laces buttons and Ribbons hookes and Eyes	3	6	4
4 lb of whale bone	0	8	0
3 pair scales and weights	1	6	6
3 old Chairs, pestle and mortar	0	5	6
69 ounces ¾ $\frac{1}{16}$ of Plate at	17	8	3
In old money and brass money	0	9	6

In the Hall house

	£	s	d
A Jack and weight	0	10	0
A fire pan, tongs, 1 pair Cobirons and other small things	0	11	0
1 tramel, 1 Iron Barr, 5 Candlesticks and 1 Cliver	0	6	0
A gun 10s. 6 lether Chairs, 1 old Chair 21s.	1	11	0
1 old Table, 2 Joynd Stooles, 1 large table chair 1 smaller	0	16	0
A parcell of Bookes 30s. a looking glass and other small things 5s. 6d.	1	15	6

In the Parlor

	£	s	d
2 pair of Cobirons brass fire pan and Tongs	0	15	0
1 livery Cupboard 1 glasskeep 1 large ovall table	1	13	0

In the Kitchin

	£	s	d
1 pair of Cobirons 1 Still 1 Jack and other small things	1	0	8
5 spitts a parcell of tinware and other small things	0	15	6
4 brasse potts and a posnett	1	4	6
A Saucepan 2 scummers 2 ladles and other small things	0	6	0
25 pewter plates	0	18	8
114½ lb of pewter of all sorts	3	13	3
One Cheese plate, 1 salver 4 skillets	0	12	6
1 old form, 1 Table and other small things	0	4	6
1 warming pan 1 frying pan 7 old Chairs	0	13	4
3 Kettles	1	15	6

In the Brewhouse

	£	s	d
2 Coppers £3 Tubbs and keelers £1 10s.	4	10	0
pailes and Lumber there	0	5	0
A parcell of Larth and timber	5	0	0
Bricks wood and other Lumber	0	10	0

In the Corne Chamber

	£	s	d
About 8 Comb of wheat	7	0	0
A parcell of decayed Clover seed	[		]
3 bushells 2 fans a Skreen 3 Shovells and a Sive	1	6	6
A Caving sive and other husbandry tooles	0	4	3
A pulling hooke Carpenters Tooles and other things	2	4	0
2 saddles and a Bridle	0	16	0

In the Cellars

	£	s	d
5 beere vessels 2 ale Stooles glass bottles and other lumber	2	1	0

In the Kitchin Chamber and Clossit

	£	s	d
1 desk a Joynd Stoole and other Small things	1	0	0
A Parcell of Books	0	15	0
1 fether bed with the bedsted and furniture to it belonging	6	0	0
1 table Cupboard 2 green Chairs 6 Stooles and other goods	0	19	0

	£	s	d
In the Parlor Chamber			
1 fetherbed with the bedsted and furniture belonging	8	3	6
1 serge Couch 2 Chairs 2 Stooles suitable	1	17	0
1 serge Counterpane 1 Cupboard cloth	1	0	0
3 wrought chairs 2 Stooles 1 Chest of drawers	1	13	0
1 ovall table cobirons fire pan tongs dogs bellows and looking glas	0	19	0
In the Passage Chamber and Clossit			
1 livery Cupboard 2 old hutches 1 hanging press and other lumber	1	3	0
In the hither Shop Chamber			
1 fether bed 2 bolsters 1 pallat bed with the furniture	3	5	11
1 blew bedsted with the furniture and other goods	1	17	6
In the further Shop Chamber			
1 fether bed with the bedsted and furniture belonging	5	2	6
1 bedsted with Curtaines Matt and Line	1	5	0
1 Large Chest 1 livery table with other goods there	1	3	0
His wearing apparrell	4	0	0
In the Garretts			
4 Leaves of a Skreen 3 oaken boards 1 Cheese Rack	0	10	0
The Linnen apprized at	5	13	10
Goods sold and debts rec'd before the apprizall	6	16	3
The mourning that Mrs. Quixley had out of the Shop	7	5	2
The mourning Mrs. Bacon had out of the Shop	1	18	8
The Crop of Barly after all Charges deducted	26	2	6¼
The debts Sperate and desperate	70	16	8
Totall	419	3	3¾[1]

[signed] Hen: Boughton
John Culpeck

[Proved 6 June 1705]

[1] The total is incorrect and should be £419 15s. 0½d, taking account of other calculations in the inventory which are incorrect and are marked by [sic].

Glossary of Historical Terms

used in the inventories on pp. 116–124

Alkinore	Presumably a kind of Dutch linen, perhaps named after a town (?Alkmaar)
Ancerins	(Antherines) A kind of poplin, a mixed woven fabric with a corded surface
Bagonet	Bayonet
Bame, Scales & Waits	Weighing beam, with scales and weights
Barratine	A coarse fabric, originally from Holland
Bay	A fabric of worsted warp and woollen weft, lightly fulled and raised. Often associated with Colchester
Belladine	A kind of silk
Bodys	Bodice
Boiler	A vessel in which a liquid was boiled
Bores laps	Probably burlaps, originally a kind of holland, later a coarse canvas
Buccoram/Bucceram	A fine linen or cotton fabric (now Buckram)
Buffet stoole	A low, wooden stool; a foot stool
Bushell	A vessel for measuring grain
Calico/Calleco	A cotton cloth, originally imported from the East (named after Calicut in India)
Callamanco	(Calamanco) A highly glazed woollen fabric, twilled and patterned (but see note 127)
Caving sive	A sieve for separating grain from chaff. 'Caving' is a dialect word meaning the husks of corn
Chafing dish	A dish placed on a container of hot charcoal or ashes, to keep food warm
Chaney/Cheney	A worsted or woollen fabric, originally from China
Clipt money	Coins which had been clipped. In the mid seventeenth century coins were in short supply and were often clipped or melted down. Milled edges on coins were first introduced in 1662 to discourage clipping.
Cliver	Cleaver or chopper
Cobirons	Fire-irons with hooks, on which a spit rested
Coole	Charcoal
Crepers	Small fire-dogs, used in pairs
Damask	A rich silk or linen fabric, with patterns and glazed surface (originally from Damascus)
Deale	Of deal (wood)
Diaper	A twilled linen fabric, woven with diamond patterns, mainly used for tablecloths, napkins, etc.
Dimety	A strong cotton fabric, with raised stripes
Dog	An iron, used in pairs, for supporting burning logs; in another sense it refers to an iron tie-bar used in building
Droper	Some kind of kitchen utensil
Drudging box	A perforated container for sprinkling powders or flour
Drugget(t)	A coarse cloth, often used for garments and floor-coverings
Eal stol	Ale stool, or stand on which a barrel rested
Ell wide	A measure of cloth, normally 45 inches
Fan	Used for winnowing
Farrendine	A fabric, said to be a mixture of silk, wool and hair
Fillittings	Strips of material for binding

125

Forrett ribbons	(Normally Ferrett) A stout tape of cotton or silk
Frieze	A coarse woollen cloth, usually with a nap on one side
Fring	Presumably an ornamental fringe
Fustian	A thick, coarse material of cotton or flax (originally from Fostat, a suburb of Cairo)
Galloone	A narrow ribbon or braid, for trimming clothes
Garlick Holland	Perhaps this refers to a place in Holland, or possibly to the plant used for its fibres, like nettles
Ghentings	A fine linen cloth, originally from Ghent
Glass keep	Cupboard with glass front, or for storage of glasses
Goche	(Gotch) A large pitcher
Grasey	Greasy
Grat	Grater
Hanger	In Tarver's case, this was presumably a belt with loops to carry a rapier; it can also be an iron bar in a chimney, from which pot-hooks were hung
Hanging press	A cupboard for hanging clothes
Hardel	Could be a version of 'handle', the wooden implement in which teasles were mounted
Heters	(Heaters) A form of smoothing-iron
Holland/Holand	Expensive and high-quality linen, originally imported from Holland
Hopes	Hops, for flavouring beer
Houndscote	Apparently a kind of 'say' cloth
Huckaback	A stout linen fabric with rough surface, suitable for towelling
Hutch(e)	A small chest, often used for storing clothes
Jack	A machine for turning a cooking-spit
Jett	A large ladle or spout
Keler/Keeler	A shallow wooden vessel for cooling liquids
Koule	(or Cowl) A large open tub used in dairies and kitchens
Laves	Could be the 'leaves' or panels of a domestic screen
Lincie-Woolcie or Woolice	A textile of mixed fibres, for example wool and flax
Livery Cupboard	A small ventilated cupboard for the storage of food and drink often for use in a chamber at night
Lyste	The border or selvage of a cloth; sometimes deliberately coloured and sewn on as a form of identification. Can also refer to types of 'bay' cloth
Matt & line	A coarse mat laced to a bed-frame with cords, to support a mattress
Meshing staf	A stick used to stir the mashing-vat in the making of beer
Meshing or Mishing tub	Mashing vat in which malt and boiling water was stirred
Mourning	Presumably clothes or bands worn in mourning a death
Niles	(Noils) Short wool left in the comb after the long fibres have been removed
Orris	A kind of patterned lace, in gold and silver
Osnabrix	A kind of coarse linen, originally from Osnabrück
Pallat bed	A straw bed
Perpetuanas/Perpetuanoes	A durable 'everlasting' cloth, often used for suiting
Pillow biers	Pillow cases
Porenger	(Porringer) A dish or bowl with lugs, used for soup, porridge, etc.
Posnett	A small metal cooking pot, with three feet and a handle
Poot	Pot
Pouls	This may refer to tufts or knots of wool

Pulling hooke	Probably an implement for cleaning wool. Thomas Infield of Nayland, a fellmonger who died in 1676, had two Pulling Chambers, each containing quantities of wool
Poudring tube	A tub for salting and pickling meat
Rapers	Rapiers
Rash	A smooth textile made of silk or worsted, often used for cloaks
Rings	Wringers
Rises	This seems to be connected with the spinning of silk
Roul	Could be a roll or roller
Sad Culerd	Usually defined as dark- or sober-coloured, but in the fifteenth to sixteenth centuries a specific colour was clearly intended
Sagitta	A woollen material, sometimes mixed with silk, often used for jackets and waistcoats
Say	A fine cheap cloth resembling serge, all wool
Sceps	Baskets
Scored	Scoured
Scummer/Skummer	(Skimmer) A shallow perforated vessel or ladle for skimming liquids
Serge	A durable twilled cloth, sometimes a mixture of worsted and wool
Shag	A cloth with a velvet nap on one side, sometimes of goat's hair
Shalloones/Sholons	A closely woven light worsted, used chiefly for linings; named after Chalons-sur-Marne
Shakel	Shackle
Shiftenen bord	A trestle-table for some unknown purpose
Skillet	A cooking pot of metal, usually with three feet and a handle
Skreen/Skrien	Can mean either a domestic screen to protect people from the fire, draught or light, or an agricultural implement for separating corn from dust
Still	As this was associated with a fireplace, it probably means a 'steel' for striking a spark; in other contexts the word refers to an apparatus for distilling cordials and medicines, or to a wooden tub
Stomacher	A tightly-fitting garment; either a kind of waistcoat worn by men or an ornamental covering for the chest worn by women
Strikeing bord	An ironing board. In Suffolk 'streek' meant 'to iron clothes'.
Stuff	Light fabric without a nap or pile; a general term for worsted fabrics
Tabby	A general term for silk taffeta
Tamarins/Tamerines	A kind of striped cloth
Tames stripes/Tamet	(Tammy) A fine worsted of good quality, often glazed
Tester	A canopy over a bed supported on posts
Toulon	From Toulon in France?
Tope	(Top) A sliver of combed wool ready for spinning
Tramel	Hooks of wrought-iron on which to hang pots
Treves	(Trevis) A beam or frame for securing an animal while being shod
Tube	Tub
Tunel	Funnel
Turkia	Turkish in origin or style
Twistin mill	A machine for twisting together several threads of yarn
Warpen mill	A revolving wooden frame, on which yarn is wound to prepare it as warp for the loom

General Index

*Illustrations in **bold** type.*

Index of Contemporary Names

A person's place of residence was Lavenham, unless otherwise stated.